Thy Kingdom Come, The Next Big Thing.

Clayton B Carlson

ISBN-10: 1988226066
ISBN-13: 978-1988226064

Published by First Page Solutions, Kelowna BC Canada

Table of Contents

CHAPTER 1

UNDERSTANDING THE

KINGDOM OF GOD

Doing Kingdom work has been a hot topic in Christian circles for quite a while now. Living out the love of God to those we encounter in the world should be the aim of every Christian. It's been said the sermon people hear the loudest is given without words. It's this sermon each of us live out every day as we become the hands and feet of Jesus. The Holy Spirit living inside of us, shows the love of God to the world by letting those around us enjoy the fruit of the spirit born out of our actions. This spiritual fruit produced inside the followers of Jesus, proclaims the Kingdom of God has started to all those we interact with.

Some Christians think they can bring the Kingdom of God to the world now, if only all Christians would work together for the good of humanity, individually doing all we can to help feed, clothe, teach and serve our fellow man. Collaborating with all who will help get the job done, they believe that God will bring his Kingdom now at this time. Through their good works, these Christians do everything they can to hasten the arrival of God's Kingdom.

Does this belief stand the test of history? There was a time, in some countries, when Christians were in control of all aspects of society and human endeavour. Despite the fact Christians were the ones in charge of major world altering societies for well over a thousand years, the Kingdom of God is still not here. If you find the thought of living a life surrounded and controlled by Christians appealing, you should look into European history from 400 AD to the mid 1700's. The intolerant atrocities we see the Christians of old commit in the name of Jesus can make us shudder. These atrocities highlight why we need to have Christ live his life within us and why love is the greatest fruit of the spirit.

It was this intolerance and persecution that drove the pilgrims out of England and Holland to start a freedom loving civilization in the New World. It's not surprising the governments those pilgrims formed in the New World had a distinct separation between church and state. This separation was of prime importance to the New World's founders. Having the same authorities running the church and state was a hard lesson learned by these immigrants and they would not have that mistake repeated in their new home. Freedom of thought, faith, movement and association to name a few, would not be surrendered.

When we look at the freedoms settlers were seeking to find in the New World, we can see how restrictive their old society was. Those who left the old world, risked life and limb for the chance to make a free new life for themselves and their children. What they tried to create in the New World highlights the societal basics they felt they could not live without. If they had been happy with the governmental model they had come from, then they would have merely duplicated it for themselves in the New World. They would not have left their familiar lives back home had they been living in anything that came close to the Kingdom of God. They deliberately made their societies secular in nature as they knew that living in a freedom loving secular society was better than in a dogmatic religious one. Living in a Christian society will not guarantee a Godly one. Technology has changed with the passing of time, but the early Christians had the same word of God we have today. For the Kingdom of God to come on earth, we will need to be full of Gods Holy Spirit dwelling inside us.

Trying to build a society today, totally governed by Christians, will produce the same bitter fruit that was harvested in the past. We have no better insight on how to overcome our human nature now than those Christians of old did. Christians today have trouble getting along with each other let alone running an entire society without being intolerant. We desperately need the fruit of the spirit, full and ripe inside of us, with God firmly in charge, if we are to have any hope of running a Godly Kingdom.

In his book, Kingdom Come, Reggie McNeal encourages the reader to get out and do good for those around them, to right the wrongs they see in their world. To do good whenever they can, in whatever way they can. He wants Christians to become instruments of change for the better in this world. To this sentiment I can only echo amen. Christians should do all of that and more. I disagree with Reggie however, on the motivation behind such outreach. In his book Reggie confidently states God's plan for humanity, "He is working in all areas of human endeavour to advance his Kingdom so that people can experience life as he intends it." I believe boldly stating that, "This work of redeeming and restoring what was lost in Eden is God's major work in the world." not to be biblically supported for this time period. Reggie makes it sound like God's plan for humanity is being frustrated by the Christians he is trying to deliver it through. Yes God does have a plan for humanity to live in his Kingdom as his beloved children, but I believe it's not for Christians to bring it to fruition during this life. It will come to us from God when he deems the time to be right.

The Kingdom of God is being brought to us in stages. The Kingdom of God has been prepared for us from the foundation of the world and God is unfolding the Kingdoms arrival according to his plan. It will be here at its full when the final enemies of death and the grave are defeated.

1Corinthians 15:21-28   Easy-to-Read Version
21 Death comes to people because of what one man did. But now there is resurrection from death because of another man. 22 I mean that in Adam all of us die. And in the same way, in Christ all of us will be made alive again. 23 But everyone will be raised to life in the right order. Christ was first to be raised. Then, when Christ comes again, those who belong to him will be raised to life. 24 Then the end will come. Christ will destroy all rulers, authorities, and powers. Then he will give the Kingdom to God the Father. 25 Christ must rule until God puts all enemies under his control. 26 The last enemy to be destroyed will be death.

27 As the Scriptures say, "God put everything under his control." When it says that "everything" is put under him, it is clear that this does not include God himself. God is the one putting everything under Christ's control. 28 After everything has been put under Christ, then the Son himself will be put under God. God is the one who put everything under Christ. And Christ will be put under God so that God will be the complete ruler over everything.

Then God will live as a father with all of his children. It is now that the Kingdom will have completely arrived for all of the conquers to enjoy. The Kingdom of God will be ushered in by God himself.

Revelation 21:1-7   The Living Bible
1 Then I saw a new earth (with no oceans!) and a new sky, for the present earth and sky had disappeared. 2 And I, John, saw the Holy City, the new Jerusalem, coming down from God out of heaven. It was a glorious sight, beautiful as a bride at her wedding. 3 I heard a loud shout from the throne saying, "Look, the home of God is now

among men, and he will live with them and they will be his people; yes, God himself will be among them. 4 He will wipe away all tears from their eyes, and there shall be no more death, nor sorrow, nor crying, nor pain. All of that has gone forever." 5 And the one sitting on the throne said, "See, I am making all things new!" And then he said to me, "Write this down, for what I tell you is trustworthy and true: 6 It is finished! I am the A and the Z—the Beginning and the End. I will give to the thirsty the springs of the Water of Life—as a gift! 7 Everyone who conquers will inherit all these blessings, and I will be his God and he will be my son.

Doing good and serving others is a Christian goal for this life. When done in love, our efforts will give glory to God. The motivation behind these altruistic acts should be for developing the fruit of the Holy Spirit within us. Having this spiritual fruit ripening inside of us is what we should be striving for. The good works we do are not to bring the Kingdom of God here to earth but are to develop us into the followers of Jesus that God wants us to become, as well as display God to those we encounter.

The dangers to our spiritual lives are made very clear to us by Jesus in his parable of the sheep and the goats. Those who do not let the holy spirit work inside of them and grow the fruit of the spirit, are literally going down a dead end road.

Matthew 25:31-46   English Standard Version
31 "When the Son of Man comes in his glory, and all the angels with him, then he will sit on his glorious throne. 32 Before him will be gathered all the nations, and he will separate people one from another as a shepherd separates the sheep from the goats. 33 And he will place the sheep on his right, but the goats on the left. 34 Then the King will say to those on his right, 'Come, you who are blessed by my Father, inherit the Kingdom prepared for you from the foundation of the world. 35 For I was hungry and you gave me food, I was thirsty and you gave me drink, I was a stranger and you welcomed me, 36 I was naked and you clothed me, I was sick and you visited me, I was in prison and you came to me.' 37 Then the righteous will answer him, saying, 'Lord,

when did we see you hungry and feed you, or thirsty and give you drink? 38 And when did we see you a stranger and welcome you, or naked and clothe you? 39 And when did we see you sick or in prison and visit you?' 40 And the King will answer them, 'Truly, I say to you, as you did it to one of the least of these my brothers, you did it to me.' 41 "Then he will say to those on his left, 'Depart from me, you cursed, into the eternal fire prepared for the devil and his angels. 42 For I was hungry and you gave me no food, I was thirsty and you gave me no drink, 43 I was a stranger and you did not welcome me, naked and you did not clothe me, sick and in prison and you did not visit me.' 44 Then they also will answer, saying, 'Lord, when did we see you hungry or thirsty or a stranger or naked or sick or in prison, and did not minister to you?' 45 Then he will answer them, saying, 'Truly, I say to you, as you did not do it to one of the least of these, you did not do it to me.' 46 And these will go away into eternal punishment, but the righteous into eternal life."

Striving for spiritual perfection is to be the priority for this life. This perfection will elude us the closer we get to it, as our remaining imperfections and shortcomings will become more obvious. It is the personal character we build that will be ultimately important in the Kingdom of God. When talking about his life Paul highlights his desire to pursue the righteous perfection found in Christ.

Philippians 3: 12-16   New Life Version
12 I do not say that I have received this or have already become perfect. But I keep going on to make that life my own as Christ Jesus made me His own. 13 No, Christian brothers, I do not have that life yet. But I do one thing. I forget everything that is behind me and look forward to that which is ahead of me. 14 My eyes are on the crown. I want to win the race and get the crown of God's call from heaven through Christ Jesus. 15 All of us who are full-grown Christians should think this way. If you do not think this way, God will show it to you. 16 So let us keep on obeying the same truth we have already been following.

Galatians describes to us what the fruit of the spirit is. These are the character traits needed in

God's Kingdom.

Galatians 5:22-23   KJV
22 But the fruit of the Spirit is love, joy, peace,
long-suffering, gentleness, goodness, faith,
23 Meekness, temperance: against such there is no
law.

The spiritual fruit that is produced within us is the
key ingredient needed when God does bring his
Kingdom to earth. We play a vital role in God's
Kingdom as Kings and Priests.

1 Peter 2:9   New International Version
9 But you are a chosen people, a royal priesthood,
a holy nation, God's special possession, that you
may declare the praises of him who called you out
of darkness into his wonderful light.

Revelations 1:6
American King James Version
6 And has made us kings and priests to God and
his Father; to him be glory and dominion for ever
and ever. Amen.

Revelations 5:10   Young's Literal Translation
10 and didst make us to our God kings and priests, and we shall reign upon the earth.'
We are not meant to be just passive occupants of Gods Kingdom. We play a key part in it, as leaders of it. We will not only be the leaders in the Kingdom, but we also will sit in judgement over the world. Having a bumper crop of spiritual fruit will be essential if we are to skilfully execute the important jobs God wants us to do in his Kingdom.

1 Corinthians 6:2 Weymouth New Testament
2Do you not know that God's people will sit in judgement upon the world? And if you are the court before which the world is to be judged, are you unfit to deal with these petty matters?

We will not only judge the world, we will also judge the angels.

1Corinthians 6:3   New Living Translation
3 Don't you realize that we will judge angels? So you should surely be able to resolve ordinary disputes in this life.

To play these key roles in the Kingdom of God we must develop into mature Christians with discernment of good and evil. The life we live now struggling against worldly temptation, in the Holy Spirit's power, is what will grow a crop of full ripe fruit. We can't afford to procrastinate in preparing for our assignments as kings and priests awaiting us in the Kingdom.

Hebrews 5:11-14   New King James Version
11 of whom we have much to say, and hard to explain, since you have become dull of hearing. 12 For though by this time you ought to be teachers, you need someone to teach you again the first principles of the oracles of God; and you have come to need milk and not solid food. 13 For everyone who partakes only of milk is unskilled in the word of righteousness, for he is a babe. 14 But solid food belongs to those who are of full age, that is, those who by reason of use have their senses exercised to discern both good and evil..

CHAPTER 2

IT'S NOT ABOUT SAVING

OURSELVES

Christianity has traditionally been focused mainly on the salvation of people. In what some see as, the great commission, Jesus told his disciples to go out into the world, make disciples, baptize and teach what he had commanded them.

Matthew 28:16-20   Common English Bible
16 Now the eleven disciples went to Galilee, to the mountain where Jesus told them to go. 17 When they saw him, they worshipped him, but some doubted. 18 Jesus came near and spoke to them, "I've received all authority in heaven and on earth. 19 Therefore, go and make disciples of all nations, baptizing them in the name of the Father and of the Son and of the Holy Spirit, 20 teaching them to obey everything that I've

commanded you. Look, I myself will be with you every day until the end of this present age."

In making salvation the main objective for their efforts it seems as though most Christians have put, getting ready for, looking forward to and proclaiming the Kingdom of God on the back burner. Jesus instructed Christians to make disciples and teach them what he has commanded them to do. Earlier in the book of Matthew, we can read one of the commands Jesus gave us. It is the same thing he did. We are to preach the gospel of the Kingdom.

Matthew 4:23 King James Version 23 And Jesus went about all Galilee, teaching in their synagogues, and preaching the gospel of the Kingdom, and healing all manner of sickness and all manner of disease among the people.

Matthew 24:13-14 American Standard Version 13 But he that endureth to the end, the same shall be saved.
14 And this gospel of the Kingdom shall be preached in the whole world for a testimony unto

all the nations; and then shall the end come.

Accepting the salvation brought by Jesus has been taught, by most of Christianity, as the main goal for Christians to reach. For we cannot be forgiven our sins without accepting the cleansing power only brought by Jesus. Diminishing the importance of preaching the gospel of the Kingdom of God and all that it entails, most Christians have turned the gospel into a message about Jesus and salvation alone. Focusing on personal safety in heaven and the avoidance of hell has left Christians without much purpose in their spiritual lives.

Seeing salvation as the primary thing needed for the Christian life, a large percentage of the new converts after receiving their salvation, stroke it off their bucket list. Getting on with life like any other non-Christian of the world, secure in their belief they have salvation waiting for them when they die. The calamities of the world can be pushed out of their minds reach as long as they and those around them are safe. They drift through the world oblivious to its sorrows focused only on their own comfort and happiness. If there was a theme song for this state of mind it would have to be "Comfortably Numb" by Pink Floyd.

This drifting through life with no goals larger than their own salvation is why I believe many Christians have developed apathy about being the hands and feet of Jesus to this world. They think they have fulfilled their spiritual obligations by accepting Jesus into their hearts, thus securing their salvation from death. Some may get a peripheral glimpse of God's plan for his Kingdom, but when they try to focus on it other things fill their vision. Thoughts of the Kingdom are replaced by images of the blissfulness of heaven, where there is little urgency for personal development just never ending peace and tranquillity. Having lost understanding of the Kingdom and what role they could be playing in it, they drift into religious comfort and conformity rather than proclaiming the Kingdom of God through their words and deeds.

Leprosy is an infectious ancient scourge on humanity. It's debilitating affects impede your ability to feel by destroying your nerves in affected areas. This numbing will make you unaware of injuries that you may incur. The disease can be easily passed on to other people. By not making the instructions of Jesus to proclaim the Kingdom of God to the world as the main purpose of Christian activity, we infect Christianity with a form of spiritual leprosy. This loss of purpose for personal growth can take us away from the heart of God, leaving us feeling nothing when God's heart is breaking.

Bill Steely recorded the song "Bother Me" as a plea to God to let his heart be bothered by what bothers God's. In it he describes how he has a problem and can't feel his heart, and it bothers him, what doesn't bother him anymore. Being healed of our spiritual leprosy is essential if we are to get a good vision of the Kingdom of God. We need the heart of God along with the fruit of his spirit if we are to fulfil his agenda for our lives. We can all sing along with Bill no matter where we are on our spiritual journey towards perfection, as it is a life long struggle.

Conformity is not a trait that those proclaiming the Kingdom of God are strong in. They are more often than not, walking off the path their societies are taking. They are usually counter cultural, adding a distinctive flavour to those they associate with. As Jesus taught, his followers are to be like salt, adding flavour and preservation to those they encounter. We are also to be shining beacons of love to the world, pointing people to God so they too can give him praise.

Matthew 5:13-16   New Century Version
13 "You are the salt of the earth. But if the salt loses its salty taste, it cannot be made salty again. It is good for nothing, except to be thrown out and walked on.14 "You are the light that gives light to the world. A city that is built on a hill cannot be hidden. 15 And people don't hide a light under a bowl. They put it on a lampstand so the light shines for all the people in the house. 16 In the same way, you should be a light for other people. Live so that they will see the good things you do and will praise your Father in heaven.

Embedded within these verses is a sober warning

to Christians who do not keep on the narrow path of righteousness. If we lose our salty taste, that is, if we grow complacent in our faith and start walking in the way of the world we cannot be made salty again. Like in the parable of the sheep and goats we will be destined for destruction. Some other scriptures that have a similar sentiment are as follows.

Luke 9:60-62 Good News Translation
60 Jesus answered, "Let the dead bury their own dead. You go and proclaim the Kingdom of God."
61 Someone else said, "I will follow you, sir; but first let me go and say good-bye to my family."
62 Jesus said to him, "Anyone who starts to plow and then keeps looking back is of no use for the Kingdom of God."

Hebrews 6:4-8   King James Version
4 For it is impossible for those who were once enlightened, and have tasted of the heavenly gift, and were made partakers of the Holy Ghost,
5 And have tasted the good word of God, and the powers of the world to come,
6 If they shall fall away, to renew them again unto

repentance; seeing they crucify to themselves the Son of God afresh, and put him to an open shame. 7 For the earth which drinketh in the rain that cometh oft upon it, and bringeth forth herbs meet for them by whom it is dressed, receiveth blessing from God:
8 But that which beareth thorns and briers is rejected, and is nigh unto cursing; whose end is to be burned.

These warnings are usually passed over by those who just seek salvation and a fast track to heaven. If we are only worried about our own welfare, it is hard to say that we love our neighbour as ourselves, let alone show the fruit of the spirit to them so they too may give praise to God.

Philippians 3:15-19 New American Standard Bible
15 Let us therefore, as many as are perfect, have this attitude; and if in anything you have a different attitude, God will reveal that also to you; 16 however, let us keep living by that same standard to which we have attained.17 Brethren, join in following my example, and observe those

who walk according to the pattern you have in us.
18 For many walk, of whom I often told you, and
now tell you even weeping, that they are enemies
of the cross of Christ, 19 whose end is destruction,
whose god is their appetite, and whose glory is in
their shame, who set their minds on earthly things.

We need to shift our focus from ourselves to those
around us. We also need to be wise about what we
believe and who we follow. If we are in doubt we
need to seek the wisdom contained in God's word
the bible and look to see what kind of fruit is
being produced in ourselves and those we
trustingly learn from.

Matthew 7:15-23 Jubilee Bible 2000
15 Keep yourselves also from the false prophets,
who come to you in sheep's clothing, but
inwardly they are ravening wolves.
16 Ye shall know them by their fruits. Do men
gather grapes of thorns, or figs of thistles?
17 Even so every good tree brings forth good
fruit, but a corrupt tree brings forth evil fruit.
18 A good tree cannot bring forth evil fruit,
neither can a corrupt tree bring forth good fruit.

19 Every tree that does not bring forth good fruit is hewn down and cast into the fire.

20 So that by their fruits ye shall know them.

21 Not every one that saith unto me, Lord, Lord, shall enter into the Kingdom of the heavens, but he that doeth the will of my Father who is in the heavens.

22 Many will say to me in that day, Lord, Lord, have we not prophesied in thy name? and in thy name have cast out devils? and in thy name done many wonderful works?

23 And then I will profess unto them, I never knew you; depart from me, ye that work iniquity.

CHAPTER 3

WHO IS GOD AND WHAT IS HIS PLAN?

As we have already read in Matthew 25:34 the Kingdom has been prepared for us from the foundation of the world. Why has it taken God so long to bring it to us? Why are we not living in it now? The answer to these questions lie in the knowledge of God's purpose for mankind. His plans for the Kingdom will fulfil his dreams and objectives. We need to start by understanding God's overall goal if we are to understand how and why the Kingdom will come.

The driving force behind all life, after self-preservation, is reproduction. Having been made in the image of God it is not hard to see how reproduction is also the desire of God. Creating humanity in his image, God did not limited us just to his physical image. It can also refer to our emotional needs, wants and desires being in the image of God's. If a child acts like their parent we could say that they were the image of their parent, and mean in personality, or temperament. In the same way, as we desire family and relationship, so does God.

Genesis 1:27 International Children's Bible
27 So God created human beings in his image. In the image of God he created them. He created them male and female.

God has no beginning and he has no end, he is eternal.

Psalm 90:2 English Standard Version
2 Before the mountains were brought forth,or ever you had formed the earth and the world,from everlasting to everlasting you are God.

Psalm 93:2 American Standard Version
2 Thy throne is established of old: Thou art from everlasting.

In John we are given more details about God. The Word is part of God and has been with God from the beginning.

John 1:1-2   Good News Translation
1 In the beginning the Word already existed; the Word was with God, and the Word was God. 2 From the very beginning the Word was with God.

It was through the Word that all things were made.

John 1:3-5   Contemporary English Version
3 And with this Word, God created all things. Nothing was made without the Word. Everything that was created 4 received its life from him, and his life gave light to everyone. 5 The light keeps shining in the dark, and darkness has never put it out.

Then the Word came into the world as Jesus, but the world did not recognize him as God.

Matthew 1:22-23 J.B. Phillips New Testament
22-23 All this happened to fulfil what the Lord

had said through the prophet—'Behold, a virgin shall be with child, and bear a son, and they shall call his name Immanuel'. ("Immanuel" means "God with us.")

John 1:10-11   Good News Translation
10 The Word was in the world, and though God made the world through him, yet the world did not recognize him. 11 He came to his own country, but his own people did not receive him.

There is one more part of God the bible describes to us, it is his Spirit. It dwells in us and directs us in the ways of God. The Spirit will also give us the power to overcome the world and do God's will in our lives. It was also by his Spirit that he created the heavens.

1 Corinthians 2:11-14 Holman Christian Standard Bible
11 For who among men knows the thoughts of a man except the spirit of the man that is in him? In the same way, no one knows the thoughts of God except the Spirit of God. 12 Now we have not received the spirit of the world, but the Spirit who

comes from God, so that we may understand what has been freely given to us by God. 13 We also speak these things, not in words taught by human wisdom, but in those taught by the Spirit, explaining spiritual things to spiritual people. 14 But the unbeliever does not welcome what comes from God's Spirit, because it is foolishness to him; he is not able to understand it since it is evaluated spiritually.

Job 26:13   New King James Version
13 By His Spirit He adorned the heavens; His hand pierced the fleeing serpent.

God had a long time to work out his plans before anything was created. He planned out the end from the beginning. He started with what he wanted to end up with, then worked backwards to have it happen. I believe that God want's children. He wants to reproduce himself. We are told that we are to become the children of God and joint heirs with Jesus. Sharing in the glory of Jesus is the end result God has in mind for all in humanity that want to become his children. The possibility of being like Jesus, as he is like God, becoming

God's children born of his Spirit, makes our upcoming transformation truly something to look forward to.

Romans 8:17   New International Version
17 Now if we are children, then we are heirs—heirs of God and co-heirs with Christ, if indeed we share in his sufferings in order that we may also share in his glory.

1John 3:2   New Life Version
2 Dear friends, we are God's children now. But it has not yet been shown to us what we are going to be. We know that when He comes again, we will be like Him because we will see Him as He is.

Hebrews 9:28   Living Bible
28 so also Christ died only once as an offering for the sins of many people; and he will come again, but not to deal again with our sins. This time he will come bringing salvation to all those who are eagerly and patiently waiting for him.

Through the Old Testament prophets, as well as in other books of the bible, God has declared his desire to live with and make those who choose to follow him his people. He desires to have a relationship with those who want to know, follow and love him he doesn't force himself onto humanity but lovingly cares for us.

Deuteronomy 30:15-20King James Version
15 See, I have set before thee this day life and good, and death and evil;
16 In that I command thee this day to love the Lord thy God, to walk in his ways, and to keep his commandments and his statutes and his judgments, that thou mayest live and multiply: and the Lord thy God shall bless thee in the land whither thou goest to possess it.
17 But if thine heart turn away, so that thou wilt not hear, but shalt be drawn away, and worship other gods, and serve them;
18 I denounce unto you this day, that ye shall surely perish, and that ye shall not prolong your days upon the land, whither thou passest over Jordan to go to possess it.
19 I call heaven and earth to record this day against you, that I have set before you life and death, blessing and cursing: therefore choose life,

that both thou and thy seed may live:

20 That thou mayest love the Lord thy God, and that thou mayest obey his voice, and that thou mayest cleave unto him: for he is thy life, and the length of thy days: that thou mayest dwell in the land which the Lord sware unto thy fathers, to Abraham, to Isaac, and to Jacob, to give them.

Ezekiel 37:27 New International Version

27 My dwelling place will be with them; I will be their God, and they will be my people.

Jeremiah 32:38 Lexham English Bible

38 And they will be for me a people, and I will be for them God.

Revelation 21:3 World English Bible

3 I heard a loud voice out of heaven saying, "Behold, God's dwelling is with people, and he will dwell with them, and they will be his people, and God himself will be with them as their God

Hosea 11:4 The Voice

4 I led them along with leather cords; with ropes of love I showed them the way. As I dealt with

them, I lifted the yoke from their neck; I bent down to give them their food.

Being holy, God will only live in a sin free environment. Sin leads to death and God is life and love. Sin over time would ultimately be harmful to God's Kingdom and try to destroy it. To have children and reproduce himself God couldn't just create a finished product if it was to have free will. Free will is a necessity, otherwise God would only be creating robots that had no other option but do what they were created to do. To have a sentient being that loved selflessly and unfailingly as God does could not be created by fiat. The new God child would have to decide for itself if it would follow in the ways of its father.

This decision process is vital for the emotional development of the God child. Making a decision demands that you have a choice to decide about. God had to develop a way for the unformed God children to be able to choose between accepting his way of love, or rejecting it. For a choice to be made there had to be sin, something that was opposite of God. This was all planned before anything was created and God was alone with his thoughts. Sin had to come from somewhere for there to be a choice made. But where would it come from?

Again God could not create sin, instead he let it run its course in the sentient spirit beings that he created. He did not create them so they would sin, but he knew that they might not choose to follow in his paths of love. Being created out of spirit they would be eternal and the choices they made would also be everlasting. They would either follow him or choose to take the path of sin that would lead, not to death, because they are spiritual beings, but to eternal imprisonment. Allowing the angels free moral agency to walk their own path shows how committed God is to free moral agency and living with only those who choose him. His ways of love lead to the full and abundant life that he wants for his family.

Now that one third of the angels turned their backs on God and chose to take their own way, the time was right for God to create humanity a little lower than the angels. Lower, by creating them as physical mortal beings, without eternal life and subject to death if they chose sin.

Psalm 8:3-9 Living Bible

3 When I look up into the night skies and see the work of your fingers—the moon and the stars you have made— 4 I cannot understand how you can bother with mere puny man, to pay any attention to him! 5 And yet you have made him only a little lower than the angels and placed a crown of glory and honor upon his head. 6 You have put him in charge of everything you made; everything is put under his authority: 7 all sheep and oxen, and wild animals too, 8 the birds and fish, and all the life in the sea. 9 O Jehovah, our Lord, the majesty and glory of your name fills the earth.

I believe that understanding the true limitations mortality places upon humanity is vital in comprehending the plan of God as well as his Kingdom. Realizing immortality and eternal life is only brought to us through the good pleasure of God in his time, frees us from the lies fed to us by Satan to misdirect us away from God and his Kingdom. A common belief throughout all of history is that mankind possesses an immortal spirit, or soul. Mankind has generally believed Satan's lie.

Genesis 3:4 Easy-to-Read Version
4 But the snake said to the woman, "You will not die.
When man was created he was created as a living soul Genesis 2:7, the original Hebrew text uses the word nephesh for soul.

Genesis 2:7 King James Version
7 And the Lord God formed man of the dust of the ground, and breathed into his nostrils the breath of life; and man became a living soul.

The King James Version translators knew that nephesh meant mortality as shown by their list of usages for the word found in the Strong's concordance. They never intended it to mean immortality. It refers only to our physical body, intellect and emotions. On its own, there is no part of us that will live on after we die physically.

נֶפֶשׁ

nephesh

neh'-fesh

From H5314; properly a breathing creature, that is, animal or (abstractly) vitality; used very widely in a literal, accommodated or figurative sense (bodily or mental)

KJV Usage: any, appetite, beast, body, breath, creature, X dead (-ly), desire, X [dis-] contented, X fish, ghost, + greedy, he, heart (-y), (hath, X jeopardy of) life (X in jeopardy), lust, man, me, mind, mortality, one, own, person, pleasure, (her-, him-, my-, thy-) self, them (your) -selves, + slay, soul, + tablet, they, thing, (X she) will, X would have it.

Later after man's sin and banishment from Eden, God sets Cherubim to keep man from eating of the tree of life and gaining eternal life. The fact that man did not have eternal life after being banished from the garden upholds the fact that we were not created with eternal life in Genesis 2:7. Had we been created with an eternal soul, we would not have had to eat from the tree of life, as immortality would already be in our possession.

Genesis 3:22-24 King James Version

22 And the Lord God said, Behold, the man is become as one of us, to know good and evil: and now, lest he put forth his hand, and take also of the tree of life, and eat, and live for ever:

23 Therefore the Lord God sent him forth from the garden of Eden, to till the ground from whence he was taken.

24 So he drove out the man; and he placed at the east of the garden of Eden Cherubims, and a flaming sword which turned every way, to keep the way of the tree of life.

Mankind is mortal and because of that we will die. The only hope we have is the promise of God to resurrect us. He will bring us back to life when it is our time. God has an orderly plan for mankind's salvation that he will bring about according to his purpose.

1Corinthians 15:21-23 Common English Bible

21 Since death came through a human being, the resurrection of the dead came through one too. 22 In the same way that everyone dies in Adam, so also everyone will be given life in Christ. 23 Each

event will happen in the right order: Christ, the first crop of the harvest, then those who belong to Christ at his coming.

CHAPTER 4

CHOOSE YOUR OWN FATE

Some may wonder, why didn't Jesus just come at the start after Adam sinned? Well if he had come back then there would not have been as many potential children for God. Before we can accept the atonement brought to us by Jesus we must first be born physically into this world. Then we can be born into the spiritual realm of God.

1Corinthians 15:42-49 New International Version 42 So will it be with the resurrection of the dead. The body that is sown is perishable, it is raised imperishable; 43 it is sown in dishonor, it is raised in glory; it is sown in weakness, it is raised in power; 44 it is sown a natural body, it is raised a spiritual body. If there is a natural body, there is also a spiritual body. 45 So it is written: "The first man Adam became a living being"; the last Adam, a life-giving spirit. 46 The spiritual did not come first, but the natural, and after that the spiritual. 47 The first man was of the dust of the earth; the second man is of heaven. 48 As was the earthly man, so are those who are of the earth; and as is the heavenly man, so also are those who are of heaven. 49 And just as we have borne the image of the earthly man, so shall we bear the image of the heavenly man.

For God to go through the pain of this spiritual child birth he would have wanted to get the best returns for his efforts. Think of the sorrows Jesus went through to redeem us of our sins. His desire is for many to share in the Kingdom. God has plans for a large family, in his house there are many rooms. All of mankind, from the start till the end, will be given their opportunity to accept the salvation Jesus alone brought for us. You might think, yes but if Jesus had brought salvation from the start, there could have been more salvation's, for we can only be saved through Jesus.

For the majority of humanity before Jesus came it is true, they could have no knowledge of Jesus. At best, the people from that time could only have trust in God and that he had a plan for their salvation. They didn't know the specifics but their unwavering faith in God, would be counted to them, the same as if they knew Jesus and the salvation he would ultimately bring to the world. They had faith in God to deliver them and that was all they knew. It wouldn't have mattered to them how God saved them, they only knew that he would. Their faith was counted to them for righteousness.

Genesis 15:6 King James Version
6 And he believed in the Lord; and he counted it to him for righteousness.

Psalm 106:31 World English Bible
31 That was credited to him for righteousness, for all generations to come.

Some believe that because the faith of the people from this time period was counted to them for righteousness that when they died they went into God's Kingdom of heaven. Were this to have been the case then the trials of Jesus would have been just for show and not real game changers for the fate of humanity. If any human had preceded Jesus into the presence of the Father before the payment was made, then why did Jesus have to come and pay for our sins? It was not a forgone conclusion that Jesus would pass all of the tests and fulfil all of the prophecies to bring about our salvation. The trials and suffering he went through were real, with dire consequences of failure for the plans of God had he not completed them. Had Jesus failed, Satan could have won the battle for humanity.

John 3:13 New Life Version
13 "No one has gone up into heaven except the One Who came down from heaven. That One is the Son of Man *Who is in heaven.

The fact that the faithful people of old are not in heaven is born out to us by the faith chapter of Hebrews 11. In this chapter we are told about the people of faith, how they trusted God and followed him into strange lands. They were always looking for their true home, the home God had promised they would share with him. They would get to this new home, his Kingdom, in the future just as he had promised them. None of them received all of the promises God had made to them. They must wait till the end when God will let them share with us, our better rewards, all at the same time. Till then they must wait for the return of Jesus.

Hebrews 11:39-40 Living Bible
39 And these men of faith, though they trusted God and won his approval, none of them received all that God had promised them; 40 for God wanted them to wait and share the even better rewards that were prepared for us.

Being mortal, without any part of them that lives on after death. They will wait with the rest of humanity for the call of God to bring them back to life. They will wait in their graves to become reanimated from the dust of the ground they returned to after death. They will be resurrected as will all who have ever lived. Some to a resurrection of eternal life and some to shame.

Daniel 12:2 Easy-to-Read Version

2 There are many who are dead and buried. Some of them will wake up and live forever, but others will wake up to shame and disgrace forever.

If you have ever tried to do something for a person that they wanted to do for themselves, you may recognize the attitude displayed by my daughter when she was a toddler. I believe the first phrase she vocalized for herself was "Me Do". I knew she would fail at the task at hand and I would need to eventually work it out for her, but until she realized that fact, all of my efforts to help would be firmly rebuffed with an emphatic "Me Do". I believe this attitude of independence within humanity is why God let mankind go their own way. We do not want help until we are sure we cannot do it ourselves. We won't embrace a Savior if we don't recognize our need for one. For the most part, from the beginning of man's creation until after Abraham, Isaac and Jacob, humanity has had little to no interest in knowing their creator. There were rare exceptions like Noah, but when it came to deciding how to live their lives the bulk of humanity was exclaiming to God "Me Do".

From Moses till the death of Jesus, God had worked with a group of people to teach them how to live lives that would lead to perfection. He gave them his law to show them what was needed and how short they came from perfection, highlighting to them their need for a Savior to save them from their sins. Laws, sacrifices and regulations were not sufficient to bring the salvation desperately needed by mankind. God had given clues, throughout his word, to the method he would use to bring that salvation, but few were to recognize it when it came.

Had humanity not gone through this period of trying their own ways to live, at their resurrection they would still believe they knew best and would reject Jesus not wanting to follow God's ways of love. Had God not given laws to live by through Moses, some would no doubt believe they could have lived an acceptable life, if God had only told them how. Now history has supplied an ample amount of witnesses who have tried to gain their own salvation by keeping the laws of God, proving that it is absolutely impossible. When humanity is resurrected and has their opportunity to accept Jesus and the atonement for sin brought only through him, they will not be able to say they could do it without him. Countless generations will be there to prove and testify that mankind is utterly incapable of living a sinless life through their own power.

Even now over two thousand years after Jesus came and died for them most of humanity lives their lives the way they think they should, with little regard to what Jesus taught. Is this majority of humanity to be lost to God? Will God not be able to have them as his children? I believe the bible shows us that he will have them as his children, if they make the choice to accept him. This opportunity to accept God's offer of redemption and become his children will happen through a resurrection. There is ultimately to be several resurrections for humanity, each one serves a different purpose, and is designed for a specific group of people.

There are nine instances given to us in the bible of a back to physical life resurrection. These include people who had died through tragedy, illness, age, or for the glory of God. All of these resurrections were back to the life they had lost. Later on, they would all ultimately die again and go to their graves.

1Kings 17:20-22 New Century Version
20 Then he prayed to the Lord: "Lord my God, this widow is letting me stay in her house. Why have you done this terrible thing to her and caused her son to die?" 21 Then Elijah lay on top of the boy three times. He prayed to the Lord, "Lord my God, let this boy live again!"22 The Lord answered Elijah's prayer; the boy began breathing again and was alive.

2Kings 4:32-36 Jubilee Bible 2000
32 And when Elisha was come into the house, behold, the child was laid dead upon his bed.
33 He went in therefore and shut the door upon both of them and prayed unto the LORD.
34 Then he went up and lay upon the child and put his mouth upon his mouth and his eyes upon his eyes and his hands upon his hands; thus he stretched himself upon the child; and the flesh of

the child waxed warm.

35 Then he returned and walked through the house to and fro and went up and stretched himself upon him again; and the child sneezed seven times, and the child opened his eyes.

36 And he called Gehazi and said, Call this Shunammite. So he called her. And as she was coming in unto him, he said, Take up thy son.

2Kings 13:20-21 Expanded Bible
20 Then Elisha died and was buried. At that time ·groups [bands] of Moabites would rob the land in the springtime. 21 Once as some Israelites were burying a man, suddenly they saw a ·group [band] of Moabites coming. The Israelites threw the dead man into Elisha's ·grave [tomb]. When the man touched Elisha's bones, the man ·came back to life [revived] and stood on his feet.

Luke 7:11-15 Amplified Bible
11 Soon afterward, Jesus went to a town called Nain, and His disciples and a great throng accompanied Him.
12 [Just] as He drew near the gate of the town, behold, a man who had died was being carried

out—the only son of his mother, and she was a widow; and a large gathering from the town was accompanying her.

13 And when the Lord saw her, He had compassion on her and said to her, Do not weep.

14 And He went forward and touched the funeral bier, and the pallbearers stood still. And He said, Young man, I say to you, arise [from death]!

15 And the man [who was] dead sat up and began to speak. And [Jesus] gave him [back] to his mother.

Luke 8:50-55 American Standard Version

50 But Jesus hearing it, answered him, Fear not: only believe, and she shall be made whole.

51 And when he came to the house, he suffered not any man to enter in with him, save Peter, and John, and James, and the father of the maiden and her mother.

52 And all were weeping, and bewailing her: but he said, Weep not; for she is not dead, but sleepeth.

53 And they laughed him to scorn, knowing that she was dead.

54 But he, taking her by the hand, called, saying,

Maiden, arise.
55 And her spirit returned, and she rose up immediately: and he commanded that something be given her to eat.

John 11:42-44 International Children's Bible
42 I know that you always hear me. But I said these things because of the people here around me. I want them to believe that you sent me." 43 After Jesus said this, he cried out in a loud voice, "Lazarus, come out!" 44 The dead man came out. His hands and feet were wrapped with pieces of cloth, and he had a cloth around his face. Jesus said to them, "Take the cloth off of him and let him go."

Matthew 27:52-53 Living Bible
52 and tombs opened, and many godly men and women who had died came back to life again. 53 After Jesus' resurrection, they left the cemetery and went into Jerusalem, and appeared to many people there.

Acts 9:36-41 The Message
36-37 Down the road a way in Joppa there was a

disciple named Tabitha, "Gazelle" in our language. She was well-known for doing good and helping out. During the time Peter was in the area she became sick and died. Her friends prepared her body for burial and put her in a cool room.

38-40 Some of the disciples had heard that Peter was visiting in nearby Lydda and sent two men to ask if he would be so kind as to come over. Peter got right up and went with them. They took him into the room where Tabitha's body was laid out. Her old friends, most of them widows, were in the room mourning. They showed Peter pieces of clothing the Gazelle had made while she was with them. Peter put the widows all out of the room. He knelt and prayed. Then he spoke directly to the body: "Tabitha, get up."

40-41 She opened her eyes. When she saw Peter, she sat up. He took her hand and helped her up. Then he called in the believers and widows, and presented her to them alive.

Acts 20:9-12 New Living Translation
9 As Paul spoke on and on, a young man named Eutychus, sitting on the windowsill, became very

drowsy. Finally, he fell sound asleep and dropped three stories to his death below. 10 Paul went down, bent over him, and took him into his arms. "Don't worry," he said, "he's alive!" 11 Then they all went back upstairs, shared in the Lord's Supper, and ate together. Paul continued talking to them until dawn, and then he left. 12 Meanwhile, the young man was taken home alive and well, and everyone was greatly relieved.

All of these people would go back to their graves and turn to dust, just as all of mankind had done before them. We are told that those who are dead are asleep. They are not aware of their surroundings, they know nothing and they are destined to be forgotten. This analogy of being asleep is used repeatedly over fifty times throughout the bible.

1Corinthians 15:17-19 King James Version
17 And if Christ be not raised, your faith is vain; ye are yet in your sins.
18 Then they also which are fallen asleep in Christ are perished.
19 If in this life only we have hope in Christ, we

are of all men most miserable.

John 11:11-13 Good News Translation
11 Jesus said this and then added, "Our friend Lazarus has fallen asleep, but I will go and wake him up."
12 The disciples answered, "If he is asleep, Lord, he will get well."
13 Jesus meant that Lazarus had died, but they thought he meant natural sleep.

Ecclesiastes 9:5 New Life Version
5 For the living know they will die. But the dead know nothing, and they will receive nothing further, for they are forgotten.

The bulk of humanity will have to wait in their graves until God decides to bring them back to life through a resurrection. This resurrection to life will not give them a second chance to know God and accept the salvation of Jesus. For the people finding themselves in this resurrection it will be the first time they have been introduced to Jesus. Being resurrected now, is the first time they will be able to clearly see and hear the message of love and life that God brings to his potential children. Contrary to popular opinion, God is not in a race with Satan to save the souls of humanity. For the vast majority of mankind, God has left them to their own ways, blinded to his paths of righteousness.

Acts 14:16 New Living Translation
16 In the past he permitted all the nations to go their own ways,

God has blinded the bulk of humanity on purpose. Most people that lived before Jesus came, as well as the people that lived after Jesus died for mankind's salvation, have had their hearts hardened. Our God is on time according to his schedule. He is not desperately trying to save the world's population on mass now before each one dies. Having a plan for humanities future resurrection, God is not in a rush to save any, as all will have their opportunity to choose. God is being careful not to lose any by accident or omission.

Isaiah 6:8-10 The Living Bible

8 Then I heard the Lord asking, "Whom shall I send as a messenger to my people? Who will go?" And I said, "Lord, I'll go! Send me." 9 And he said, "Yes, go. But tell my people this: 'Though you hear my words repeatedly, you won't understand them. Though you watch and watch as I perform my miracles, still you won't know what they mean.' 10 Dull their understanding, close their ears, and shut their eyes. I don't want them to see or to hear or to understand, or to turn to me to heal them."

Romans 11:8 The Voice
8 The Scriptures continue to say it best: God has confounded them so they are not able to think, given them eyes that do not see, and ears that do not hear, Down to this very day.
There are a few people that will seek out God on their own, those who do he will hear and draw them to himself.

James 4:8 New International Version
8 Come near to God and he will come near to you. Wash your hands, you sinners, and purify your hearts, you double-minded.

As when Jesus healed the daughter of the Syrophoenician Woman, God will respond to those who come to him in faith.

Mark 7:27-29 Living Bible
27 Jesus told her, "First I should help my own family—the Jews. It isn't right to take the children's food and throw it to the dogs."
28 She replied, "That's true, sir, but even the puppies under the table are given some scraps from the children's plates."
29 "Good!" he said. "You have answered well—so well that I have healed your little girl. Go on home, for the demon has left her!"

We are told by Jesus we can only get to the father through him. This is a founding pillar of Christianity, there is salvation in no other name. No other way could be found for salvation when Jesus was weeping in Gethsemane before his crucifixion,

Matthew 26:39 The Message
39 Going a little ahead, he fell on his face,

praying, "My Father, if there is any way, get me out of this. But please, not what I want. You, what do you want?"

But there was no other way back then and there is still no other way for salvation today. Having faith, keeping the law, sacrificing animals, nothing can save us. Mankind, past, present and future must go through Jesus to obtain the redemption of sin. Without the sacrifice of Jesus being paid for our sins, we could not have our sins covered. Mankind had no cleansing until after Jesus completed his work on the cross.

God would not accept an IOU from humanity because Jesus was coming to redeem us. The price of our redemption had to be paid first, in full, in blood. It was only after this payment had been made could we receive a covering for our sin. Until then we were still under the old covenant, the new covenant power was displayed with the tearing of the temple veil, symbolizing mankind's access to God had arrived.

Hebrews 9:11-28 New International Version

11 But when Christ came as high priest of the good things that are now already here, he went through the greater and more perfect tabernacle that is not made with human hands, that is to say, is not a part of this creation. 12 He did not enter by means of the blood of goats and calves; but he entered the Most Holy Place once for all by his own blood, thus obtaining eternal redemption. 13 The blood of goats and bulls and the ashes of a heifer sprinkled on those who are ceremonially unclean sanctify them so that they are outwardly clean. 14 How much more, then, will the blood of Christ, who through the eternal Spirit offered himself unblemished to God, cleanse our consciences from acts that lead to death, so that we may serve the living God!

15 For this reason Christ is the mediator of a new covenant, that those who are called may receive the promised eternal inheritance—now that he has died as a ransom to set them free from the sins committed under the first covenant.

16 In the case of a will, it is necessary to prove the death of the one who made it, 17 because a will is in force only when somebody has died; it never takes effect while the one who made it is living.

18 This is why even the first covenant was not put into effect without blood. 19 When Moses had proclaimed every command of the law to all the people, he took the blood of calves, together with water, scarlet wool and branches of hyssop, and sprinkled the scroll and all the people. 20 He said, "This is the blood of the covenant, which God has commanded you to keep." 21 In the same way, he sprinkled with the blood both the tabernacle and everything used in its ceremonies. 22 In fact, the law requires that nearly everything be cleansed with blood, and without the shedding of blood there is no forgiveness.

23 It was necessary, then, for the copies of the heavenly things to be purified with these sacrifices, but the heavenly things themselves with better sacrifices than these. 24 For Christ did not enter a sanctuary made with human hands that was only a copy of the true one; he entered heaven itself, now to appear for us in God's presence. 25 Nor did he enter heaven to offer himself again and again, the way the high priest enters the Most Holy Place every year with blood that is not his own. 26 Otherwise Christ would have had to suffer many times since the creation

of the world. But he has appeared once for all at the culmination of the ages to do away with sin by the sacrifice of himself. 27 Just as people are destined to die once, and after that to face judgment, 28 so Christ was sacrificed once to take away the sins of many; and he will appear a second time, not to bear sin, but to bring salvation to those who are waiting for him.

Christianity's fundamental principle of no salvation without Jesus, is the very reason why those faithful believers who died, before Jesus paid the price for sin, could not be in heaven with God immediately after they died. They would have to wait until the new covenant had arrived. Being wholly mortal, they are waiting in their graves like all of the believers before and after them. Waiting to receive the fulfilment of God's promises to them at the return of Jesus.

1Corinthians 15:6
Disciples' Literal New Testament
6 After that He appeared to over five-hundred brothers at-one-time, of whom the majority are remaining until now. But some fell-asleep.

Except for those few who pursue God by their own volition, people coming to God within the new covenant time are responding to the call of God in their lives. Jesus explained that God would have to draw people to him so that they may be saved. God specifically calls those he has chosen for a purpose. He chooses the cast offs of society, the ones who are the least, to display his power to the mighty. With our shortcomings to keep us humble we do the work God has called us for, in the power of his Holy Spirit.

John 6:44 Good News Translation
44 People cannot come to me unless the Father who sent me draws them to me; and I will raise them to life on the last day.

John 6:65 Easy-to-Read Version
65 Jesus said, "That is why I said, 'Anyone the Father does not help to come to me cannot come.'"

1Corinthians 1:26-29 Good News Translation
26 Now remember what you were, my friends,

when God called you. From the human point of view few of you were wise or powerful or of high social standing. 27 God purposely chose what the world considers nonsense in order to shame the wise, and he chose what the world considers weak in order to shame the powerful. 28 He chose what the world looks down on and despises and thinks is nothing, in order to destroy what the world thinks is important. 29 This means that no one can boast in God's presence.

Ephesians 2:4-10   New Life Version
4 But God had so much loving-kindness. He loved us with such a great love. 5 Even when we were dead because of our sins, He made us alive by what Christ did for us. You have been saved from the punishment of sin by His loving-favor. 6 God raised us up from death when He raised up Christ Jesus. He has given us a place with Christ in the heavens. 7 He did this to show us through all the time to come the great riches of His loving-favor. He has shown us His kindness through Christ Jesus.
8 For by His loving-favor you have been saved from the punishment of sin through faith. It is not

by anything you have done. It is a gift of God. 9 It is not given to you because you worked for it. If you could work for it, you would be proud. 10 We are His work. He has made us to belong to Christ Jesus so we can work for Him. He planned that we should do this.

CHAPTER 5

RESPONDING TO THE CALL

OF GOD

Being called by God, repenting and starting to follow Jesus is just the first steps for the new Christian. We receive the Holy Spirit as a grantee of our adoption at baptism and from then on our life long goal is to follow his lead towards perfection.

Philippians 1:6 God's Word Translation
6 I'm convinced that God, who began this good work in you, will carry it through to completion on the day of Christ Jesus.

Ephesians 1:12-14 The voice
12 As a result, we—the first to place our hope in the Anointed One—will live in a way to bring Him glory and praise. 13 Because you, too, have

heard the word of truth—the good news of your salvation—and because you believed in the One who is truth, your lives are marked with His seal. This is none other than the Holy Spirit who was promised 14 as the guarantee toward the inheritance we are to receive when He frees and rescues all who belong to Him. To God be all praise and glory!

Jesus prayed that his followers would become as one just as he and his father were one. We are all to become one together through the Holy Spirit dwelling within us. The world will glorify God by his Spirit dwelling in us and producing fruit.

John 17:20-26 Easy-to Read Version
20 "I pray not only for these followers but also for those who will believe in me because of their teaching. 21 Father, I pray that all who believe in me can be one. You are in me and I am in you. I pray that they can also be one in us. Then the world will believe that you sent me. 22 I have given them the glory that you gave me. I gave them this glory so that they can be one, just as you and I are one. 23 I will be in them, and you will be

in me. So they will be completely one. Then the world will know that you sent me and that you loved them just as you loved me. 24 "Father, I want these people you have given me to be with me in every place I am. I want them to see my glory—the glory you gave me because you loved me before the world was made. 25 Father, you are the one who always does what is right. The world does not know you, but I know you, and these followers of mine know that you sent me. 26 I showed them what you are like, and I will show them again. Then they will have the same love that you have for me, and I will live in them."

Those who are called by God in this life have a special mission to accomplish for the Kingdom of God. We need to keep our focus on the goals that lie before us, not getting side tracked by the cares of this world. As we have seen earlier, God has called us to be kings, priests and judges in his Kingdom. Our success as the children of God depends on us developing the fruit of the spirit during this life. Being led by the spirit, we develop it's fruit by serving those around us. The prime reason for serving others is to increase the fruit developing within us. We serve others, not to bring the Kingdom of God to the world, but to give the world a taste of the coming Kingdom and refine the fruit growing inside us.

How does the fruit of the spirit grow inside of us so we can overcome the world and go on to the good works God has for us to do? The answer is as easy as it is hard. We need to follow where his Spirit leads us. It might be something you are passionate about, it may be something that makes you mad, or it breaks your heart and you want it changed. Whatever your "it" is remember that love is the most important fruit of them all. Your quest doesn't need to be a seemingly great one in the eyes of others, for it is personal character development that we need to accomplish. We cannot develop this character in isolation, we must let our light shine to others, as we preach the Kingdom and make disciples.

Growing the fruit of patience for example doesn't require us to grow it on the other side of the world handing out food to hungry people. It can be developed in your own home every time you have to wait for a family member. It's in the everyday repetition that you develop the strongest muscles, developing the fruit of the spirit is similar. Everyday life gives us ample opportunity to develop fruit if we pray for guidance and transform our minds as we try to act like Jesus while being sensitive to the promptings of God in service to others.

Romans 12:2 New Century Version
2 Do not be shaped by this world; instead be changed within by a new way of thinking. Then you will be able to decide what God wants for you; you will know what is good and pleasing to him and what is perfect.

Titus 3:5 Jubilee Bible 2000
5 not by works of righteousness which we have done, but according to his mercy he saved us, by the washing of regeneration and renewing of the Holy Spirit,

James 1:27 International Children's Bible
27 Religion that God the Father accepts is this: caring for orphans or widows who need help; and

keeping yourself free from the world's evil influence. This is the kind of religion that God accepts as pure and good.

The Kingdom of God is coming in stages. Jesus came to the people of world and proclaimed that the Kingdom had arrived among them. This was the beginning of mankind's redemption. Like a mustard seed that starts out small and grows into the largest garden plant, starting off small the Kingdom of God will eventually fill the whole world.

Luke 17:20-21 The Message
20-21 Jesus, grilled by the Pharisees on when the Kingdom of God would come, answered, "The Kingdom of God doesn't come by counting the days on the calendar. Nor when someone says, 'Look here!' or, 'There it is!' And why? Because God's Kingdom is already among you."

Matthew 13:31-32 New International Version
31 He told them another parable: "The Kingdom of heaven is like a mustard seed, which a man took and planted in his field. 32 Though it is the

smallest of all seeds, yet when it grows, it is the largest of garden plants and becomes a tree, so that the birds come and perch in its branches."

Later Jesus described preaching about the Kingdom of God as the reason why he came to the earth. The arrival of the Kingdom has been planned out by God from before creation. It is through the coming Kingdom's stages that the children of God are born.

Luke 4:42-43 Living Bible
42 Early the next morning he went out into the desert. The crowds searched everywhere for him, and when they finally found him, they begged him not to leave them but to stay at Capernaum. 43 But he replied, "I must preach the Good News of the Kingdom of God in other places too, for that is why I was sent."

With his resurrection, Jesus became the first born of many brethren. He leads us, showing what is possible. We will follow his example and be resurrected at his return.

Romans 8:29-30 Modern English Version
29 For those whom He foreknew, He predestined to be conformed to the image of His Son, so that He might be the firstborn among many brothers. 30 And those whom He predestined, He also called; and those whom He called, He also justified; and those whom He justified, He also glorified.

Those who overcome this world will be transformed into the spiritual likeness of Jesus for we will be like him. Responding to God's call, those that accept Jesus in this life will be born as sons and daughters into the family of God. Through the developing impregnation of the Spirit, Jesus will be in us, as he is in God, and together we all will become the children of God. Along with Jesus we will be the first fruits of God's children.

1John 3:1-2 King James Version
3 Behold, what manner of love the Father hath bestowed upon us, that we should be called the sons of God: therefore the world knoweth us not, because it knew him not.

2 Beloved, now are we the sons of God, and it doth not yet appear what we shall be: but we know that, when he shall appear, we shall be like him; for we shall see him as he is.

Philippians 3:20-21 New International Version
20 But our citizenship is in heaven. And we eagerly await a Savior from there, the Lord Jesus Christ, 21 who, by the power that enables him to bring everything under his control, will transform our lowly bodies so that they will be like his glorious body.

Philippians 3:21 Names of God Bible
21 Through his power to bring everything under his authority, he will change our humble bodies and make them like his glorified body.

Colossians 3:4 Lexham English Bible
4 When Christ, who is your life, is revealed, then you also will be revealed with him in glory.

James 1:18 Common English Bible
18 He chose to give us birth by his true word, and here is the result: we are like the first crop from

the harvest of everything he created.

John 14:18-20 New International Reader's Version
18 I will not leave you like children who don't have parents. I will come to you. 19 Before long, the world will not see me anymore. But you will see me. Because I live, you will live also. 20 On that day you will realize that I am in my Father. You will know that you are in me, and I am in you.

Believers have always wanted to know when they will be transformed into their Spiritual life. Our resurrection takes place at the return of Jesus. At his return all that are his will be raised to join him in the air as he comes back to the world as it's sovereign king. This is the next big event to happen for Christians. The followers of Jesus asked him when they would be born into spirit life. In John 6 Jesus repeatedly and plainly gave them the answer, our transformation will take place at the last day.

John 6:39 New International Version

39 And this is the will of him who sent me, that I shall lose none of all those he has given me, but raise them up at the last day.

John 6:40 Living Bible
40 For it is my Father's will that everyone who sees his Son and believes on him should have eternal life—that I should raise him at the Last Day."

John 6:44 King James Version
44 No man can come to me, except the Father which hath sent me draw him: and I will raise him up at the last day.

John 6:54 Modern English Version
54 Whoever eats My flesh and drinks My blood has eternal life. And I will raise him up on the last day.

We are given more information about the last day in 1 Thessalonians. Here, the birth of those called by God and have overcome the world, is being described to us. We will meet him in the air at his return just as he promised. Those that are asleep will rise first, followed by the saints that are alive at his coming.

1 Thessalonians 4:16-17 New Century Version
16 The Lord himself will come down from heaven with a loud command, with the voice of the archangel, and with the trumpet call of God. And those who have died believing in Christ will rise first. 17 After that, we who are still alive will be gathered up with them in the clouds to meet the Lord in the air. And we will be with the Lord forever.

Those who are called by God to come to him have their opportunity for salvation now in this life. They would have been better off had they not known about Jesus, than turn away from him after receiving their salvation.

2 Peter 2:20-22 International Children's Bible
20 They were made free from the evil in the world by knowing our Lord and Savior Jesus Christ. But if they return to evil things and those things control them, then it is worse for them than it was before. 21 Yes, it would be better for them to have

never known the right way. That would be better than to know the right way and then to turn away from the holy teaching that was given to them. 22 What they did is like this true saying: "A dog eats what it throws up." And, "After a pig is washed, it goes back and rolls in the mud."

Those who half half-heartedly follow God will be like the unwise virgins who ran out of oil in their lamps. This parable of Jesus doesn't paint a very rosy future for them.

Matthew 25:1-13 Darby Translation
1 Then shall the Kingdom of the heavens be made like to ten virgins that having taken their torches, went forth to meet the bridegroom.
2 And five of them were prudent and five foolish.
3 They that were foolish took their torches and did not take oil with them;
4 but the prudent took oil in their vessels with their torches.
5 Now the bridegroom tarrying, they all grew heavy and slept.
6 But in [the] middle of [the] night there was a cry, Behold, the bridegroom; go forth to meet

him.

7 Then all those virgins arose and trimmed their torches.

8 And the foolish said to the prudent, Give us of your oil, for our torches are going out.

9 But the prudent answered saying, [We cannot,] lest it might not suffice for us and for you. Go rather to those that sell, and buy for yourselves.

10 But as they went away to buy, the bridegroom came, and the [ones that were] ready went in with him to the wedding feast, and the door was shut.

11 Afterwards come also the rest of the virgins, saying, Lord, Lord, open to us;

12 but he answering said, Verily I say unto you, I do not know you.

13 Watch therefore, for ye know not the day nor the hour.

Perhaps this is why we are admonished to count the cost of following Jesus. We are promised that the road will not be easy, we will have to forsake everything else in this world and put God firmly foremost in our lives.

Luke 14:26-33 Good News Translation

26 "Those who come to me cannot be my disciples unless they love me more than they love father and mother, wife and children, brothers and sisters, and themselves as well. 27 Those who do not carry their own cross and come after me cannot be my disciples. 28 If one of you is planning to build a tower, you sit down first and figure out what it will cost, to see if you have enough money to finish the job. 29 If you don't, you will not be able to finish the tower after laying the foundation; and all who see what happened will make fun of you. 30 'You began to build but can't finish the job!' they will say. 31 If a king goes out with ten thousand men to fight another king who comes against him with twenty thousand men, he will sit down first and decide if he is strong enough to face that other king. 32 If he isn't, he will send messengers to meet the other king to ask for terms of peace while he is still a long way off. 33 In the same way," concluded Jesus, "none of you can be my disciple unless you give up everything you have.

Matthew 7:13-14 Living Bible
13 "Heaven can be entered only through the

narrow gate! The highway to hell is broad, and its gate is wide enough for all the multitudes who choose its easy way. 14 But the Gateway to Life is small, and the road is narrow, and only a few ever find it.

All who God calls to Jesus now need to take their salvation seriously. This is their time to make it sure, now is their day for salvation.

2Peter 1:3-11 King James Version
3 According as his divine power hath given unto us all things that pertain unto life and godliness, through the knowledge of him that hath called us to glory and virtue:
4 Whereby are given unto us exceeding great and precious promises: that by these ye might be partakers of the divine nature, having escaped the corruption that is in the world through lust.
5 And beside this, giving all diligence, add to your faith virtue; and to virtue knowledge;
6 And to knowledge temperance; and to temperance patience; and to patience godliness;
7 And to godliness brotherly kindness; and to brotherly kindness charity.
8 For if these things be in you, and abound, they

make you that ye shall neither be barren nor unfruitful in the knowledge of our Lord Jesus Christ.

9 But he that lacketh these things is blind, and cannot see afar off, and hath forgotten that he was purged from his old sins.

10 Wherefore the rather, brethren, give diligence to make your calling and election sure: for if ye do these things, ye shall never fall:

11 For so an entrance shall be ministered unto you abundantly into the everlasting Kingdom of our Lord and Saviour Jesus Christ.

2Corinthians 6:1-2 New International Version

1 As God's co-workers we urge you not to receive God's grace in vain. 2 For he says, "In the time of my favor I heard you, and in the day of salvation I helped you." I tell you, now is the time of God's favor, now is the day of salvation.

Jesus told us how we could recognize those who would not be part of his Kingdom and what their fate will be. We must not only be wise and build our future on the sure foundation of Jesus, we must also follow the Spirit where it leads being sure to develop his fruit.

Matthew 7:15-27 J.B. Phillips New Testament
15-20 "Be on your guard against false religious
teachers, who come to you dressed up as sheep
but are really greedy wolves. You can tell them
by their fruit. Do you pick a bunch of grapes from
a thorn-bush or figs from a clump of thistles?
Every good tree produces good fruit, but a bad
tree produces bad fruit. A good tree is incapable
of producing bad fruit, and a bad tree cannot
produce good fruit. The tree that fails to produce
good fruit is cut down and burnt. So you may
know men by their fruit."
21 "It is not everyone who keeps saying to me
'Lord, Lord' who will enter the Kingdom of
Heaven, but the man who actually does my
Heavenly Father's will.
22-23 "In 'that day' many will say to me, 'Lord,
Lord, didn't we preach in your name, didn't we
cast out devils in your name, and do many great
things in your name?' Then I shall tell them
plainly, 'I have never known you. Go away from
me, you have worked on the side of evil!'"
24-25 "Everyone then who hears these words of

mine and puts them into practice is like a sensible man who builds his house on the rock. Down came the rain and up came the floods, while the winds blew and roared upon that house—and it did not fall because its foundations were on the rock.

26-27 "And everyone who hears these words of mine and does not follow them can be compared with a foolish man who built his house on sand. Down came the rain and up came the floods, while the winds blew and battered that house till it collapsed, and fell with a great crash."

The struggles we go through in this life, to obtain our awaiting glory, are well worth it.

Romans 8:18 King James Version
18 For I reckon that the sufferings of this present time are not worthy to be compared with the glory which shall be revealed in us.

Those who do not turn aside, but build on the foundation of Jesus Christ will have their work tested by fire when Jesus returns. Some will suffer loss but still have life, others will receive rewards for their good works as well as have eternal life.

1Corinthians 3: 10-15 Easy-to-Read Version
10 Like an expert builder I built the foundation of that house. I used the gift that God gave me to do this. Other people are building on that foundation. But everyone should be careful how they build. 11 The foundation that has already been built is Jesus Christ, and no one can build any other foundation. 12 People can build on that foundation using gold, silver, jewels, wood, grass, or straw. 13 But the work that each person does will be clearly seen, because the Day will make it plain. That Day will appear with fire, and the fire will test everyone's work. 14 If the building they put on the foundation still stands, they will get their reward. 15 But if their building is burned up, they will suffer loss. They will be saved, but it will be like someone escaping from a fire.

CHAPTER 6

JESUS RETURNS

Leading up to the return of Jesus the world goes through many trials. Since Jesus left over two thousand years ago, people have often thought things were so bad that the return of Jesus must be immanent. Church leaders have tried to predict when his return would be and how the events unfold in detail. There are not any specific dates given in the bible for the return of Jesus. If there were, people would be sure to be on their best behaviour when that day came. Knowing the day was far in the future others would lose their urgency about getting ready. That is why his return will be like a thief in the night. For those called by God, our time to prepare for the return of Jesus is in the life we live now. For once we are dead our work of storing up treasure in heaven is over, our time for making deposits will have come to an end.

1Thessalonians 5:1-3 The Message

1-3 I don't think, friends, that I need to deal with the question of when all this is going to happen. You know as well as I that the day of the Master's coming can't be posted on our calendars. He won't call ahead and make an appointment any more than a burglar would. About the time everybody's walking around complacently, congratulating each other—"We've sure got it made! Now we can take it easy!"—suddenly everything will fall apart. It's going to come as suddenly and inescapably as birth pangs to a pregnant woman.

Matthew 6:19-21 The Voice

19 Some people store up treasures in their homes here on earth. This is a shortsighted practice— don't undertake it. Moths and rust will eat up any treasure you may store here. Thieves may break into your homes and steal your precious trinkets. 20 Instead, put up your treasures in heaven where moths do not attack, where rust does not corrode, and where thieves are barred at the door. 21 For where your treasure is, there your heart will be

also.

Although the date for the return of Jesus is not spelled out, the bible does give us an overview of major world governments that will precede the second coming of Jesus. As we look back in history we can see the rise and fall of these empires. We can gain some insight as to how close to the return of Jesus we may be if we can see how far we have already come. Danial 2 tells us of four Kingdoms that come to power. The first one was Nebuchadnezzar of Babylon, followed by three more. There are different interpretations for which Kingdom was likened to which metal.

Daniel 2:31-45 New King James Version
31 "You, O king, were watching; and behold, a great image! This great image, whose splendor was excellent, stood before you; and its form was awesome. 32 This image's head was of fine gold, its chest and arms of silver, its belly and thighs of bronze, 33 its legs of iron, its feet partly of iron and partly of clay. 34 You watched while a stone was cut out without hands, which struck the image on its feet of iron and clay, and broke them in

pieces. 35 Then the iron, the clay, the bronze, the silver, and the gold were crushed together, and became like chaff from the summer threshing floors; the wind carried them away so that no trace of them was found. And the stone that struck the image became a great mountain and filled the whole earth.

36 "This is the dream. Now we will tell the interpretation of it before the king. 37 You, O king, are a king of kings. For the God of heaven has given you a Kingdom, power, strength, and glory; 38 and wherever the children of men dwell, or the beasts of the field and the birds of the heaven, He has given them into your hand, and has made you ruler over them all—you are this head of gold. 39 But after you shall arise another Kingdom inferior to yours; then another, a third Kingdom of bronze, which shall rule over all the earth. 40 And the fourth Kingdom shall be as strong as iron, inasmuch as iron breaks in pieces and shatters everything; and like iron that crushes, that Kingdom will break in pieces and crush all the others. 41 Whereas you saw the feet and toes, partly of potter's clay and partly of iron, the Kingdom shall be divided; yet the strength of the

iron shall be in it, just as you saw the iron mixed with ceramic clay. 42 And as the toes of the feet were partly of iron and partly of clay, so the Kingdom shall be partly strong and partly fragile. 43 As you saw iron mixed with ceramic clay, they will mingle with the seed of men; but they will not adhere to one another, just as iron does not mix with clay. 44 And in the days of these kings the God of heaven will set up a Kingdom which shall never be destroyed; and the Kingdom shall not be left to other people; it shall break in pieces and consume all these Kingdoms, and it shall stand forever. 45 Inasmuch as you saw that the stone was cut out of the mountain without hands, and that it broke in pieces the iron, the bronze, the clay, the silver, and the gold—the great God has made known to the king what will come to pass after this. The dream is certain, and its interpretation is sure."

Later in Danial 7 the Kingdoms are related to beasts coming out of the sea. Further information is contained in Danial 8. Most scholars believe that the fourth empire represents the Roman Empire.

Daniel 7:1-28 Living Bible

1 One night during the first year of Belshazzar's reign over the Babylonian Empire, Daniel had a dream and he wrote it down. This is his description of what he saw:

2 In my dream I saw a great storm on a mighty ocean, with strong winds blowing from every direction. 3 Then four huge animals came up out of the water, each different from the other. 4 The first was like a lion, but it had eagle's wings! And as I watched, its wings were pulled off so that it could no longer fly, and it was left standing on the ground, on two feet, like a man; and a man's mind was given to it. 5 The second animal looked like a bear with its paw raised, ready to strike. It held three ribs between its teeth, and I heard a voice saying to it, "Get up! Devour many people!" 6 The third of these strange animals looked like a leopard, but on its back it had wings like those of birds, and it had four heads! And great power was given to it over all mankind.

7 Then, as I watched in my dream, a fourth animal rose up out of the ocean, too dreadful to describe and incredibly strong. It devoured some of its

victims by tearing them apart with its huge iron teeth, and others it crushed beneath its feet. It was far more brutal and vicious than any of the other animals, and it had ten horns.

8 As I was looking at the horns, suddenly another small horn appeared among them, and three of the first ones were yanked out, roots and all, to give it room; this little horn had a man's eyes and a bragging mouth.

9 I watched as thrones were put in place and the Ancient of Days—the Almighty God—sat down to judge. His clothing was as white as snow, his hair like whitest wool. He sat upon a fiery throne brought in on flaming wheels, and 10 a river of fire flowed from before him. Millions of angels ministered to him, and hundreds of millions of people stood before him, waiting to be judged. Then the court began its session, and the books were opened.

11 As I watched, the brutal fourth animal was killed and its body handed over to be burned because of its arrogance against Almighty God and the boasting of its little horn. 12 As for the other three animals, their Kingdoms were taken from them, but they were allowed to live a short

time longer.

13 Next I saw the arrival of a Man—or so he seemed to be—brought there on clouds from heaven; he approached the Ancient of Days and was presented to him. 14 He was given the ruling power and glory over all the nations of the world, so that all people of every language must obey him. His power is eternal—it will never end; his government shall never fall.

15 I was confused and disturbed by all I had seen (Daniel wrote in his report), 16 so I approached one of those standing beside the throne and asked him the meaning of all these things, and he explained them to me.

17 "These four huge animals," he said, "represent four kings who will someday rule the earth. 18 But in the end the people of the Most High God shall rule the governments of the world forever and forever."

19 Then I asked about the fourth animal, the one so brutal and shocking, with its iron teeth and brass claws that tore men apart and stamped others to death with its feet. 20 I asked, too, about the ten horns and the little horn that came up afterward and destroyed three of the others—the

horn with the eyes and the loud, bragging mouth, the one that was stronger than the others. 21 For I had seen this horn warring against God's people and winning, 22 until the Ancient of Days came and opened his court and vindicated his people, giving them worldwide powers of government.

23 "This fourth animal," he told me, "is the fourth world power that will rule the earth. It will be more brutal than any of the others; it will devour the whole world, destroying everything before it. 24 His ten horns are ten kings that will rise out of his empire; then another king will arise, more brutal than the other ten, and will destroy three of them. 25 He will defy the Most High God and wear down the saints with persecution, and he will try to change all laws, morals, and customs. God's people will be helpless in his hands for three and a half years.

26 "But then the Ancient of Days will come and open his court of justice and take all power from this vicious king, to consume and destroy it until the end. 27 Then all nations under heaven and their power shall be given to the people of God; they shall rule all things forever, and all rulers shall serve and obey them."

28 That was the end of the dream. When I awoke, I was greatly disturbed, and my face was pale with fright, but I told no one what I had seen.

Daniel 8:1-27 New Century Version
1 During the third year of King Belshazzar's rule, I, Daniel, saw another vision, which was like the first one. 2 In this vision I saw myself in the capital city of Susa, in the area of Elam. I was standing by the Ulai Canal 3 when I looked up and saw a male sheep standing beside the canal. It had two long horns, but one horn was longer and newer than the other. 4 I watched the sheep charge to the west, the north, and the south. No animal could stand before him, and none could save another animal from his power. He did whatever he wanted and became very powerful. 5 While I was watching this, I saw a male goat come from the west. This goat had one large horn between his eyes that was easy to see. He crossed over the whole earth so fast that his feet hardly touched the ground.
6 In his anger the goat charged the sheep with the two horns that I had seen standing by the canal. 7 I watched the angry goat attack the sheep and

break the sheep's two horns. The sheep was not strong enough to stop it. The goat knocked the sheep to the ground and then walked all over him. No one was able to save the sheep from the goat, 8 so the male goat became very great. But when he was strong, his big horn broke off and four horns grew in place of the one big horn. Those four horns pointed in four different directions and were easy to see.

9 Then a little horn grew from one of those four horns, and it became very big. It grew to the south, the east, and toward the beautiful land of Judah. 10 That little horn grew until it reached to the sky. It even threw some of the army of heaven to the ground and walked on them! 11 That little horn set itself up as equal to God, the Commander of heaven's armies. It stopped the daily sacrifices that were offered to him, and the Temple, the place where people worshiped him, was pulled down. 12 Because there was a turning away from God, the people stopped the daily sacrifices. Truth was thrown down to the ground, and the horn was successful in everything it did.

13 Then I heard a holy angel speaking. Another holy angel asked the first one, "How long will the

things in this vision last—the daily sacrifices, the turning away from God that brings destruction, the Temple being pulled down, and the army of heaven being walked on?"

14 The angel said to me, "This will happen for twenty-three hundred evenings and mornings. Then the holy place will be repaired."

15 I, Daniel, saw this vision and tried to understand what it meant. In it I saw someone who looked like a man standing near me. 16 And I heard a man's voice calling from the Ulai Canal: "Gabriel, explain the vision to this man."

17 Gabriel came to where I was standing. When he came close to me, I was very afraid and bowed facedown on the ground. But Gabriel said to me, "Human being, understand that this vision is about the time of the end."

18 While Gabriel was speaking, I fell into a deep sleep with my face on the ground. Then he touched me and lifted me to my feet. 19 He said, "Now, I will explain to you what will happen in the time of God's anger. Your vision was about the set time of the end.

20 "You saw a male sheep with two horns, which are the kings of Media and Persia. 21 The male

goat is the king of Greece, and the big horn between its eyes is the first king. 22 The four horns that grew in the place of the broken horn are four Kingdoms. Those four Kingdoms will come from the nation of the first king, but they will not be as strong as the first king.

23 "When the end comes near for those Kingdoms, a bold and cruel king who tells lies will come. This will happen when many people have turned against God. 24 This king will be very powerful, but his power will not come from himself. He will cause terrible destruction and will be successful in everything he does. He will destroy powerful people and even God's holy people. 25 This king will succeed by using lies and force. He will think that he is very important. He will destroy many people without warning; he will try to fight even the Prince of princes! But that cruel king will be destroyed, and not by human power.

26 "The vision that has been shown to you about these evenings and mornings is true. But seal up the vision, because those things won't happen for a long time."

27 I, Daniel, became very weak and was sick for

several days after that vision. Then I got up and went back to work for the king, but I was very upset about the vision. I didn't understand what it meant.

The book of Revelations describes another beast coming out of the sea and coming up out of the earth in chapters 13 and 17, with its destruction in the lake of fire in chapter 19.

Revelation 13 King James Version
1 And I stood upon the sand of the sea, and saw a beast rise up out of the sea, having seven heads and ten horns, and upon his horns ten crowns, and upon his heads the name of blasphemy.
2 And the beast which I saw was like unto a leopard, and his feet were as the feet of a bear, and his mouth as the mouth of a lion: and the dragon gave him his power, and his seat, and great authority.
3 And I saw one of his heads as it were wounded to death; and his deadly wound was healed: and all the world wondered after the beast.
4 And they worshipped the dragon which gave power unto the beast: and they worshipped the

beast, saying, Who is like unto the beast? who is able to make war with him?

5 And there was given unto him a mouth speaking great things and blasphemies; and power was given unto him to continue forty and two months.

6 And he opened his mouth in blasphemy against God, to blaspheme his name, and his tabernacle, and them that dwell in heaven.

7 And it was given unto him to make war with the saints, and to overcome them: and power was given him over all kindreds, and tongues, and nations.

8 And all that dwell upon the earth shall worship him, whose names are not written in the book of life of the Lamb slain from the foundation of the world.

9 If any man have an ear, let him hear.

10 He that leadeth into captivity shall go into captivity: he that killeth with the sword must be killed with the sword. Here is the patience and the faith of the saints.

11 And I beheld another beast coming up out of the earth; and he had two horns like a lamb, and he spake as a dragon.

12 And he exerciseth all the power of the first

beast before him, and causeth the earth and them which dwell therein to worship the first beast, whose deadly wound was healed.

13 And he doeth great wonders, so that he maketh fire come down from heaven on the earth in the sight of men,

14 And deceiveth them that dwell on the earth by the means of those miracles which he had power to do in the sight of the beast; saying to them that dwell on the earth, that they should make an image to the beast, which had the wound by a sword, and did live.

15 And he had power to give life unto the image of the beast, that the image of the beast should both speak, and cause that as many as would not worship the image of the beast should be killed.

16 And he causeth all, both small and great, rich and poor, free and bond, to receive a mark in their right hand, or in their foreheads:

17 And that no man might buy or sell, save he that had the mark, or the name of the beast, or the number of his name.

18 Here is wisdom. Let him that hath understanding count the number of the beast: for it is the number of a man; and his number is Six

hundred threescore and six.

Revelation 17 New International Version
1 One of the seven angels who had the seven bowls came and said to me, "Come, I will show you the punishment of the great prostitute, who sits by many waters. 2 With her the kings of the earth committed adultery, and the inhabitants of the earth were intoxicated with the wine of her adulteries."
3 Then the angel carried me away in the Spirit into a wilderness. There I saw a woman sitting on a scarlet beast that was covered with blasphemous names and had seven heads and ten horns. 4 The woman was dressed in purple and scarlet, and was glittering with gold, precious stones and pearls. She held a golden cup in her hand, filled with abominable things and the filth of her adulteries. 5 The name written on her forehead was a mystery: babylon the great the mother of prostitutes and of the abominations of the earth.
6 I saw that the woman was drunk with the blood of God's holy people, the blood of those who bore testimony to Jesus.
When I saw her, I was greatly astonished. 7 Then

the angel said to me: "Why are you astonished? I will explain to you the mystery of the woman and of the beast she rides, which has the seven heads and ten horns. 8 The beast, which you saw, once was, now is not, and yet will come up out of the Abyss and go to its destruction. The inhabitants of the earth whose names have not been written in the book of life from the creation of the world will be astonished when they see the beast, because it once was, now is not, and yet will come.

9 "This calls for a mind with wisdom. The seven heads are seven hills on which the woman sits. 10 They are also seven kings. Five have fallen, one is, the other has not yet come; but when he does come, he must remain for only a little while. 11 The beast who once was, and now is not, is an eighth king. He belongs to the seven and is going to his destruction.

12 "The ten horns you saw are ten kings who have not yet received a Kingdom, but who for one hour will receive authority as kings along with the beast. 13 They have one purpose and will give their power and authority to the beast. 14 They will wage war against the Lamb, but the Lamb will triumph over them because he is Lord of

lords and King of kings—and with him will be his called, chosen and faithful followers."
15 Then the angel said to me, "The waters you saw, where the prostitute sits, are peoples, multitudes, nations and languages. 16 The beast and the ten horns you saw will hate the prostitute. They will bring her to ruin and leave her naked; they will eat her flesh and burn her with fire. 17 For God has put it into their hearts to accomplish his purpose by agreeing to hand over to the beast their royal authority, until God's words are fulfilled. 18 The woman you saw is the great city that rules over the kings of the earth."

Revelation 19:20 New Living Translation
20 And the beast was captured, and with him the false prophet who did mighty miracles on behalf of the beast—miracles that deceived all who had accepted the mark of the beast and who worshiped his statue. Both the beast and his false prophet were thrown alive into the fiery lake of burning sulfur.

Most people link these prophesies together to reveal the origins of the beast that fights Jesus at his return. There is much speculation as to the identity of the prostitute who rides the beast. I will refrain from speculation and leave you to your own research and decisions. Most, who give these verses some thought, agree that we are now very close to the end times. With that in mind, every day we are alive could be our last and our next thought would be after Jesus returns to the earth. Whether the world is close to the end is really immaterial to us as Christians. It can be interesting to speculate about prophesy and to know all mysteries, as long as we don't let this speculation divert us away from the important things of our Christian life, like having love as our most prized spiritual fruit.

1Corinthians 13:1-13 Living Bible
1 If I had the gift of being able to speak in other languages without learning them and could speak in every language there is in all of heaven and earth, but didn't love others, I would only be making noise. 2 If I had the gift of prophecy and knew all about what is going to happen in the future, knew everything about everything, but didn't love others, what good would it do? Even if

I had the gift of faith so that I could speak to a mountain and make it move, I would still be worth nothing at all without love. If I gave everything I have to poor people, and if I were burned alive for preaching the Gospel but didn't love others, it would be of no value whatever.

4 Love is very patient and kind, never jealous or envious, never boastful or proud, 5 never haughty or selfish or rude. Love does not demand its own way. It is not irritable or touchy. It does not hold grudges and will hardly even notice when others do it wrong. 6 It is never glad about injustice, but rejoices whenever truth wins out. 7 If you love someone, you will be loyal to him no matter what the cost. You will always believe in him, always expect the best of him, and always stand your ground in defending him.

8 All the special gifts and powers from God will someday come to an end, but love goes on forever. Someday prophecy and speaking in unknown languages and special knowledge— these gifts will disappear. 9 Now we know so little, even with our special gifts, and the preaching of those most gifted is still so poor. 10 But when we have been made perfect and

complete, then the need for these inadequate special gifts will come to an end, and they will disappear.

11 It's like this: when I was a child I spoke and thought and reasoned as a child does. But when I became a man my thoughts grew far beyond those of my childhood, and now I have put away the childish things. 12 In the same way, we can see and understand only a little about God now, as if we were peering at his reflection in a poor mirror; but someday we are going to see him in his completeness, face-to-face. Now all that I know is hazy and blurred, but then I will see everything clearly, just as clearly as God sees into my heart right now.

13 There are three things that remain—faith, hope, and love—and the greatest of these is love.

The bible does tell us what it will be like in the end times. It will be a time of great tribulation and trial. It will be a time unparalleled in earth's history for its dangers to life and limb. Mankind will be on the brink of extinction and we would destroy all life on earth, if God doesn't step in to save us. We are told that God will step in to save humanity and he does it to save those whom he has called to Jesus, the elect of the world.

Mark 13:19-20 Modern English Version
19 For in those days there will be distress as has not been from the beginning of the creation which God created to this time, nor ever shall be.
20 "Except the Lord shortened the days, no flesh would be saved. But for the sake of the elect, whom He chose, He shortened the days.

Matthew 24:21-22 BRG Bible
21 For then shall be great tribulation, such as was not since the beginning of the world to this time, no, nor ever shall be.
22 And except those days should be shortened, there should no flesh be saved: but for the elect's sake those days shall be shortened.

Where I grew up, we had limited radio reception with only one or two stations. I would listen to the songs and change some of the words around in my head so that they would have a better message and more meaning to me. I became aware of these verses shortly before the band Queen had their hit song, We Are The Champions. Other than the first couple of lines to the second verse which I always muddle up, I think it is a great song for Christians. We have our struggles but, "we must keep going on and on and on. Because we are the champions of the world." If life is to survive we are the ones God will be saving it for. So, "there's no time for losers, caus we are the champions of the world."

Some people believe that this time of distress, this time of great tribulation, is described in Daniel 9:27 and that it will last for seven years, when applying the year for a day principle.

Daniel 9:27 New Life Version
27 That ruler will make a strong agreement with many for one week. But when half that time is past, he will put a stop to burnt gifts and grain gifts. And a very sinful man-made god will be put there. It will stay there until the one who put it there is destroyed."

Notice that the sacrifices are not cut off until the middle of the week, leaving only three and a half days of conflict. Some believe this ties in with the ministry of Jesus being only three and a half years long, culminating with his crucifixion being carried out in the middle of the literal week. If this prophecy applies to the Anti-Christ the trouble does not start until the middle of the week leaving a three and a half year period for the tribulation troubles to be endured.

Other verses are more specific, they tell us the tribulation will last for three and a half years.

Daniel 12:7 Living Bible
7 He replied, with both hands lifted to heaven, taking oath by him who lives forever and ever, that they will not end until three and a half years after the power of God's people has been crushed.

The two witnesses are the ones speaking God's truth to the Beast power during the tribulation. They will be doing this work of God for three and a half years.

Revelation 11:3 King James Version
3 And I will give power unto my two witnesses, and they shall prophesy a thousand two hundred

and threescore days, clothed in sackcloth.

The beast is the terror of the world during the tribulation. He has power for three and a half years.

Revelation 13:5 Amplified Bible
5 And the beast was given the power of speech, uttering boastful and blasphemous words, and he was given freedom to exert his authority and to exercise his will during forty-two months (three and a half years).

Those who are against God will have control for three and a half years.

Revelation 11:2 Easy-to-Read Version
2 But don't measure the yard outside the temple. Leave it alone. It has been given to those who are not God's people. They will show their power over the holy city for 42 months.

When looking at all of the scriptures it appears to me that the tribulation, a time of sorrow like never before, will last for three and a half years.

However long you think the tribulation is, it will be a time when God shows his power to the world in a mightier way than he has ever showed it to humanity before. The followers of Jesus will possibly be singing the upbeat song "It's The End Of The World" by R.E.M. as they see the return of Jesus unfold. These omnipotent displays will culminate with the return of Jesus in majesty and power.

Matthew 24:30 New Living Translation
30 And then at last, the sign that the Son of Man is coming will appear in the heavens, and there will be deep mourning among all the peoples of the earth. And they will see the Son of Man coming on the clouds of heaven with power and great glory.

Revelation 16:1-13 Living Bible
1 And I heard a mighty voice shouting from the temple to the seven angels, "Now go your ways and empty out the seven flasks of the wrath of God upon the earth." 2 So the first angel left the temple and poured out his flask over the earth, and horrible, malignant sores broke out on

everyone who had the mark of the Creature and was worshiping his statue. 3 The second angel poured out his flask upon the oceans, and they became like the watery blood of a dead man; and everything in all the oceans died. 4 The third angel poured out his flask upon the rivers and springs and they became blood. 5 And I heard this angel of the waters declaring, "You are just in sending this judgment, O Holy One, who is and was, 6 for your saints and prophets have been martyred and their blood poured out upon the earth; and now, in turn, you have poured out the blood of those who murdered them; it is their just reward." 7 And I heard the angel of the altar say, "Yes, Lord God Almighty, your punishments are just and true." 8 Then the fourth angel poured out his flask upon the sun, causing it to scorch all men with its fire. 9 Everyone was burned by this blast of heat, and they cursed the name of God who sent the plagues—they did not change their mind and attitude to give him glory. 10 Then the fifth angel poured out his flask upon the throne of the Creature from the sea, and his Kingdom was plunged into darkness. And his subjects gnawed their tongues in anguish, 11 and cursed the God of heaven for their pains and sores, but they refused to repent of all their evil deeds. 12 The sixth angel poured out his flask upon the great River Euphrates and it dried up so that the kings from the east could march their armies westward without hindrance. 13 And I saw three evil spirits disguised as frogs leap from the mouth of the Dragon, the Creature, and his False Prophet.

The trumpet will sound and Jesus will descend from heaven. Those who are his will rise from their graves to meet him in the air, then those of his that are still alive will have their turn and be changed in the twinkling of an eye into their spiritual-physical bodies. These last ones will not taste death but shall be changed from physical life into spiritual-physical eternal life.

1Thessalonians 4:15-17 New King James
15 For this we say to you by the word of the Lord, that we who are alive and remain until the coming of the Lord will by no means precede those who are asleep. 16 For the Lord Himself will descend from heaven with a shout, with the voice of an archangel, and with the trumpet of God. And the

dead in Christ will rise first. 17 Then we who are alive and remain shall be caught up together with them in the clouds to meet the Lord in the air. And thus we shall always be with the Lord.

CHAPTER 7

WHO'S THE BOSS

This is where a lot of people go off the rails on how the Kingdom of God comes to earth. They think that now Jesus and his followers return back to heaven and live there worshipping God for the rest of eternity. Being Christians this is a pleasing thought as they will be saved. But what about those who are not Christians because they died not hearing about Jesus either due to geographic location, born at the wrong time, or untimely death? The fact that, to be saved, we must decide to accept the covering sacrifice brought to humanity by Jesus, leaves those people out of the family of God. We need not fear for them, as God has a time of resurrection planned just for them. As we will see, they will have their day of salvation. But they will need to wait safely in their graves a little while longer. Fortunately when you are asleep you are blissfully unaware of the passing of time. When they are brought back to life, it will be their next thought.

Jesus does not return to heaven, but rather continues his descent to earth with all his newly born brothers and sisters. Jesus and the heavenly armies do battle with the Beast and the armies of all the nations who rally together fighting him for control of the world. This battle will be fought at Armagedon.

Revelation 16:14-21 Darby Translation
14 for they are [the] spirits of demons, doing signs; which go out to the kings of the whole habitable world to gather them together to the war of [that] great day of God the Almighty.
15 (Behold, I come as a thief. Blessed [is] he that watches and keeps his garments, that he may not walk naked, and that they [may not] see his shame.)
16 And he gathered them together to the place called in Hebrew, Armagedon.
17 And the seventh poured out his bowl on the air; and there came out a great voice from the temple of the heaven, from the throne, saying, It is

done.

18 And there were lightnings, and voices, and thunders; and there was a great earthquake, such as was not since men were upon the earth, such an earthquake, so great.

19 And the great city was [divided] into three parts; and the cities of the nations fell: and great Babylon was remembered before God to give her the cup of the wine of the fury of his wrath.

20 And every island fled, and mountains were not found;

21 and a great hail, as of a talent weight, comes down out of the heaven upon men; and men blasphemed God because of the plague of hail, for the plague of it is exceeding great.

The victorious Jesus has the Beast and the false prophet thrown into the lake of fire. John describes the battle for us in Revelations.

Revelation 19:11-21 Good News Translation

11 Then I saw heaven open, and there was a white horse. Its rider is called Faithful and True; it is with justice that he judges and fights his battles.

12 His eyes were like a flame of fire, and he wore many crowns on his head. He had a name written

on him, but no one except himself knows what it is. 13 The robe he wore was covered with blood. His name is "The Word of God." 14 The armies of heaven followed him, riding on white horses and dressed in clean white linen. 15 Out of his mouth came a sharp sword, with which he will defeat the nations. He will rule over them with a rod of iron, and he will trample out the wine in the wine press of the furious anger of the Almighty God. 16 On his robe and on his thigh was written the name: "King of kings and Lord of lords." 17 Then I saw an angel standing on the sun. He shouted in a loud voice to all the birds flying in midair: "Come and gather together for God's great feast! 18 Come and eat the flesh of kings, generals, and soldiers, the flesh of horses and their riders, the flesh of all people, slave and free, great and small!" Then I saw the beast and the kings of the earth and their armies gathered to fight against the one who was riding the horse and against his army. 20 The beast was taken prisoner, together with the false prophet who had performed miracles in his presence. (It was by those miracles that he had deceived those who had the mark of the beast and those who had worshiped the image of the beast.) The beast and the false prophet were both thrown alive into the lake of fire that burns with sulfur. 21 Their armies were killed by the sword that comes out of the mouth of the one who was riding the horse; and all the birds ate all they could of their flesh.

Revelations 14:14-20 World English Bible
14 I looked, and behold, a white cloud; and on the cloud one sitting like a son of man, having on his head a golden crown, and in his hand a sharp sickle. 15 Another angel came out of the temple, crying with a loud voice to him who sat on the cloud, "Send your sickle, and reap; for the hour to reap has come; for the harvest of the earth is ripe!" 16 He who sat on the cloud thrust his sickle on the earth, and the earth was reaped. 17 Another angel came out of the temple which is in heaven. He also had a sharp sickle. 18 Another angel came out from the altar, he who has power over fire, and he called with a great voice to him who had the sharp sickle, saying, "Send your sharp sickle, and gather the clusters of the vine of the earth, for the earth's grapes are fully ripe!" 19 The angel thrust his sickle into the earth, and gathered the

vintage of the earth, and threw it into the great wine press of the wrath of God. 20 The wine press was trodden outside of the city, and blood came out of the wine press, even to the bridles of the horses, as far as one thousand six hundred stadia.

CHAPTER 8

A TIME TO HEAL

Now fully in control of the world and its remaining population Jesus unveils the next chapter of the Kingdom of God. This new chapter will last for a thousand years. It will be a thousand years of peace and development. Satan and the demons will be locked away in a bottomless pit unable to influence mankind to do evil.

Revelation 20:1-3 Names of God Bible
1 I saw an angel coming down from heaven, holding the key to the bottomless pit and a large chain in his hand. 2 He overpowered the serpent, that ancient snake, named Devil and Satan. The angel chained up the serpent for 1,000 years. 3 He threw it into the bottomless pit. The angel shut and sealed the pit over the serpent to keep it from deceiving the nations anymore until the 1,000 years were over. After that it must be set free for a

little while.

The thousand years will be a time of healing for the world which will need restoring after the legacy left behind by mankind. The tribulation further degrades the earths capacity to sustain life, making the healing waters flowing from Jerusalem a joyous relief for the war weary world.

Ezekiel 47:8-9 King James Version
8 Then said he unto me, These waters issue out toward the east country, and go down into the desert, and go into the sea: which being brought forth into the sea, the waters shall be healed.
9 And it shall come to pass, that every thing that liveth, which moveth, whithersoever the rivers shall come, shall live: and there shall be a very great multitude of fish, because these waters shall come thither: for they shall be healed; and every thing shall live whither the river cometh.

The Holy Spirit gives us a foretaste of the glorious future we will have as the children of God which we are born as at the return of Jesus.

2Corinthians 5:1-5 The Message
1-5 For instance, we know that when these bodies
of ours are taken down like tents and folded away,
they will be replaced by resurrection bodies in
heaven—God-made, not handmade—and we'll
never have to relocate our "tents" again.
Sometimes we can hardly wait to move—and so
we cry out in frustration. Compared to what's
coming, living conditions around here seem like a
stopover in an unfurnished shack, and we're tired
of it! We've been given a glimpse of the real
thing, our true home, our resurrection bodies! The
Spirit of God whets our appetite by giving us a
taste of what's ahead. He puts a little of heaven in
our hearts so that we'll never settle for less.

Now shortly after his return all of nature and the
earth has it's turn at rejuvenation. The freedom
found in Jesus will not only be a blessing to us,
but to the entire world.

Romans 8:20-23 Living Bible
20-21 For on that day thorns and thistles, sin,
death, and decay—the things that overcame the
world against its will at God's command—will all

disappear, and the world around us will share in the glorious freedom from sin which God's children enjoy. 22 For we know that even the things of nature, like animals and plants, suffer in sickness and death as they await this great event. 23 And even we Christians, although we have the Holy Spirit within us as a foretaste of future glory, also groan to be released from pain and suffering. We, too, wait anxiously for that day when God will give us our full rights as his children, including the new bodies he has promised us— bodies that will never be sick again and will never die.

The absence of Satan does not mean that all those who live during the thousand years will choose to follow in God's way of love. Before the angels chose to rebel they lived with God in love, but one third of them chose to reject his way of love. They went their own way as will some of the people during this time. I believe that during this thousand year period those who decide to follow God will be born into his spiritual family. Those who decide to reject God and die will have to wait in their graves for a later resurrection. Having had their opportunity to accept God but rejecting him, no further opportunity will be available to them for salvation, all people at this time will have their eyes opened to God and the salvation of Jesus. Without Satan to lead them astray, there will be no reason to not follow God unless they just aren't interested.

It is with the people who live during the thousand years of worldwide restoration that the newly begotten children of God will get their first taste of service. We are to be Kings, priests and Judges in the Kingdom of God, to take on those roles there must be people who lead and help. We will be put to work right away exercising the spiritual fruits we developed running our race now, during this life.

Revelation 20:6 Living Bible
6 Blessed and holy are those who share in the First Resurrection. For them the Second Death holds no terrors, for they will be priests of God and of Christ, and shall reign with him a thousand years.

We will be with these people, lovingly leading them in the path of righteousness.

Isaiah 30:18-22 BRG Bible

18 ¶ And therefore will the Lord wait, that he may be gracious unto you, and therefore will he be exalted, that he may have mercy upon you: for the Lord is a God of judgment: blessed are all they that wait for him.

19 For the people shall dwell in Zion at Jerusalem: thou shalt weep no more: he will be very gracious unto thee at the voice of thy cry; when he shall hear it, he will answer thee.

20 And though the Lord give you the bread of adversity, and the water of affliction, yet shall not thy teachers be removed into a corner any more, but thine eyes shall see thy teachers:

21 And thine ears shall hear a word behind thee, saying, This is the way, walk ye in it, when ye turn to the right hand, and when ye turn to the left.

22 Ye shall defile also the covering of thy graven images of silver, and the ornament of thy molten images of gold: thou shalt cast them away as a menstruous cloth; thou shalt say unto it, Get thee hence.

At times we may have to scold them like children, to get their attention, before they will follow in God's way. They will learn how to live in peace, but they will have to choose to live in love.

Ezekiel 37:23 New International Version
23 They will no longer defile themselves with their idols and vile images or with any of their offenses, for I will save them from all their sinful backsliding, and I will cleanse them. They will be my people, and I will be their God.

Zechariah 14:16-17 The Voice
The day of the Eternal One is coming. It is a day of judgment when a great final battle is fought. Jerusalem and her people are under attack; and the city, it seems, falls to her enemies. But ultimately, God's people do not fight alone. The Lord comes—commanding the army of heaven—to rescue and defend His people. Ultimately, He is crowned King over all the earth. In that day, Jerusalem is transformed and reinstated as God's holy city; it becomes the center of the world, the source of life-giving waters. Even her enemies

make pilgrimages to Jerusalem to worship and adore the one True God.

16 In days to come, all people who took up arms against Jerusalem and survived will make a choice: they will either journey to Jerusalem every year to keep the Feast of Booths and to worship the King—the Eternal, Commander of heavenly armies— 17 or the families of nations will refuse the journey to Jerusalem to adore the King, the Eternal, Commander of heavenly armies. The rains will never come to those who refuse the journey.

That they may be My people and I may be their God, "says the Lord God." They will only be God's people. He will remain as their God, the only true God there is.

Jeremiah 31:33 New King James Version
33 But this is the covenant that I will make with the house of Israel after those days, says the Lord: I will put My law in their minds, and write it on their hearts; and I will be their God, and they shall be My people.

To change the relationship with God and become one of his children, they must be born by his Holy Spirit. It is Jesus and the Holy Spirit that we as their Kings, Priests and Judges are guiding them towards. God wants all who will accept Jesus to become his children.

Romans 8:14-15 New Life Version
14 All those who are led by the Holy Spirit are sons of God. 15 You should not act like people who are owned by someone. They are always afraid. Instead, the Holy Spirit makes us His sons, and we can call to Him, "My Father."

The thousand years plays a crucial part of bringing God's Kingdom to the earth. It not only gives the remnant left alive, after the beast and false prophet are defeated at the battle of Armageddon, their opportunity to accept Jesus, it also is used as a time of healing for the world and nature. Remember that the world would have been destroyed had it not been for God cutting the time short. The following generations of the survivors will go on to help repair and rebuild the earth. It has to be ready for the next resurrection group to come.

This next group will need homes and a way to survive when God brings them back from the dead. Unlike those resurrected at the return of Jesus, this group will be resurrected back into their mortal bodies as they have not had their chance to decide if they want to follow Jesus or not. Being mortal humans they will receive the reward they choose, life eternal as children of God, or death for the rest of time.

Job 19:25-27 New International Version
25 I know that my redeemer lives, that in the end he will stand on the earth.
26 And after my skin has been destroyed, yet in my flesh I will see God;
27 I myself will see him with my own eyes—I, and not another. How my heart yearns within me!

CHAPTER 9

I SET BEFORE YOU A CHOICE

CHOOSE LIFE

THAT YOU MAY LIVE

When the thousand years is over the rest of the dead, or all of humanity that has lived not being able to know Jesus, will now have their turn to decide if they will accept the sacrifice of Jesus or not. The circumstances why they did not have a chance for salvation will vary between people. Whether they had no one to teach them about Jesus where they lived, they may have died as an infant not being mentally equipped to understand salvation, or they lived before Jesus brought salvation to the world. Perhaps their eyes were blinded to redemption by God, whatever the reason for them not having the opportunity to accept Jesus while they were alive the first time, this resurrection provides them their chance to choose Jesus and his redeeming sacrifice.

John 12:37-40 Wycliffe Bible
37 And when he had done so many miracles before them [Soothly when he had done so many signs, or miracles, before them], they believed not in him;
38 that the word of Esaias, the prophet, should be fulfilled, which he said, Lord, who hath believed to our hearing, and to whom is the arm of the Lord showed?
39 Therefore they might not believe, for again Esaias said,
40 He hath blinded their eyes, and hath made hard the heart of them [and he hath endured, or made hard, the heart of them], that they see not with eyes, and understand [not] with heart; and that they be converted, and I heal them

They will get to live a lifetime without Satan distracting them away from God. Should they decide not to join the God family they will have no one to blame but themselves. They will be masters of their own fate. God will not coheres people into his family, if you don't want to be there he won't force you to be.

Verse five is a bit confusing with where the translators placed the period. The rest of the dead are not the ones in the first resurrection. The people who are in the first resurrection are blessed and holy, they are the ones who were tortured for their faith in God. They are the ones who reigned with Jesus as kings and priests for the thousand years. The rest of the dead are from the vast array of mankind that have ever lived.

Revelation 20:4-6 New King James Version
The Saints Reign with Christ 1,000 Years
4 And I saw thrones, and they sat on them, and judgment was committed to them. Then I saw the souls of those who had been beheaded for their witness to Jesus and for the word of God, who had not worshiped the beast or his image, and had not received his mark on their foreheads or on their hands. And they lived and reigned with Christ for a thousand years. 5 But the rest of the dead did not live again until the thousand years were finished. This is the first resurrection. 6 Blessed

and holy is he who has part in the first resurrection. Over such the second death has no power, but they shall be priests of God and of Christ, and shall reign with Him a thousand years.

I find that numbering the resurrections is problematic to start with. You need to specify your starting point beforehand. For instance, the first resurrection could be the one that took place in 1Kings 17:20-22, after that there would be five more before Jesus has his turn. And what about the resurrection of Jesus? We are told that he was the first born of many brethren. Shouldn't his be the first resurrection? Hopefully you can see my point. I believe that the first resurrection as used, is describing the first mass resurrection of people back to eternal life at the return of Jesus. The rest of the dead are now resurrected back to a mortal life so they can make their choice of spiritual eternal life or death.

They will not have to make a snap decision about their fate, God is not a high pressure salesman pushing you to buy his product on the spot. He wants children that are fully committed to him and his ways of love. The decisions made must last for eternity no matter what, Like in a marriage ceremony, only there is no, till death do us part clause. There can be no hesitation or questioning the decision later. To give them ample opportunity they will have a full lifetime of one hundred years. Like in the thousand years before, the children of God will be working with this vast group of humanity helping them find their way to Jesus.

Isaiah 65:17-20 Good News Translation
17 The Lord says, "I am making a new earth and new heavens. The events of the past will be completely forgotten. 18 Be glad and rejoice forever in what I create. The new Jerusalem I make will be full of joy, and her people will be happy. 19 I myself will be filled with joy because of Jerusalem and her people. There will be no weeping there, no calling for help. 20 Babies will no longer die in infancy, and all people will live out their life span. Those who live to be a hundred will be considered young. To die before that would be a sign that I had punished them.

This resurrection is not only for the people of Israel but for all of mankind.

Ezekiel 37:1-14 New King James Version
1 The hand of the Lord came upon me and brought me out in the Spirit of the Lord, and set me down in the midst of the valley; and it was full of bones. 2 Then He caused me to pass by them all around, and behold, there were very many in the open valley; and indeed they were very dry. 3 And He said to me, "Son of man, can these bones live?"
So I answered, "O Lord God, You know."
4 Again He said to me, "Prophesy to these bones, and say to them, 'O dry bones, hear the word of the Lord! 5 Thus says the Lord God to these bones: "Surely I will cause breath to enter into you, and you shall live. 6 I will put sinews on you and bring flesh upon you, cover you with skin and put breath in you; and you shall live. Then you shall know that I am the Lord."'"
7 So I prophesied as I was commanded; and as I prophesied, there was a noise, and suddenly a rattling; and the bones came together, bone to bone. 8 Indeed, as I looked, the sinews and the

flesh came upon them, and the skin covered them over; but there was no breath in them.

9 Also He said to me, "Prophesy to the breath, prophesy, son of man, and say to the breath, 'Thus says the Lord God: "Come from the four winds, O breath, and breathe on these slain, that they may live."'" 10 So I prophesied as He commanded me, and breath came into them, and they lived, and stood upon their feet, an exceedingly great army. 11 Then He said to me, "Son of man, these bones are the whole house of Israel. They indeed say, 'Our bones are dry, our hope is lost, and we ourselves are cut off!' 12 Therefore prophesy and say to them, 'Thus says the Lord God: "Behold, O My people, I will open your graves and cause you to come up from your graves, and bring you into the land of Israel. 13 Then you shall know that I am the Lord, when I have opened your graves, O My people, and brought you up from your graves. 14 I will put My Spirit in you, and you shall live, and I will place you in your own land. Then you shall know that I, the Lord, have spoken it and performed it," says the Lord.'"

We know that the house of Israel is not the only

ones brought back in this resurrection because the ones who fight God after Satan is released are not part of Israel. Not all of humanity will want to accept Jesus and choose God's ways. As the angels before them some will follow their own path. Their desire for sin is intensified when Satan is released from his prison for a little season.

Revelation 20:7-9 New King James Version
7 Now when the thousand years have expired, Satan will be released from his prison 8 and will go out to deceive the nations which are in the four corners of the earth, Gog and Magog, to gather them together to battle, whose number is as the sand of the sea. 9 They went up on the breadth of the earth and surrounded the camp of the saints and the beloved city. And fire came down from God out of heaven and devoured them.

God's Kingdom is almost completely here. Just one more battle. This is the war to end all wars, it will be the final battle mankind will wage against their creator. Those people that thought they could defeat God are themselves destroyed. At the end of this battle Satan and his demons will be thrown into the lake of fire, prepared for them, to be tormented forever.

Matthew 25:41 New Century Version
41 "Then the King will say to those on his left, 'Go away from me. You will be punished. Go into the fire that burns forever that was prepared for the devil and his angels.

In my opinion verse 10 of Revelation 20 gets translated poorly in most bibles. It is often worded as if the beast and false prophet are alive in the lake of fire and will be tormented along with Satan and the demons for ever and ever. As you can see from the interlinear bible the word "are" is in italics meaning it has been added to the text. Being mortal men they will be burned up and die when they are thrown into the lake of fire. Satan is an immortal spirit not able to die. Therefore, he and the demons will suffer for their evil choices eternally. The ashes of the beast and false prophet are there, in the lake of fire, but they as thinking living beings, are dead and gone. "Were", as in past tense, might be a better choice than the word "are", as in present tense.

Revelation 20:10 Greek Interlinear Bible NT
10 and the devil that deceived them was cast into
the lake of fire and brimstone, where the beast and
the false prophet [are], and shall be tormented day
and night for ever and ever
This final resurrection is for those who had their
opportunity to come to Jesus, or had their faith
accounted unto them as righteousness. But for
some reason they ended up rejecting the offer or
leaving the race and disqualified themselves by
their actions.

John 12:42-43 The Message
42-43 On the other hand, a considerable number
from the ranks of the leaders did believe. But
because of the Pharisees, they didn't come out in
the open with it. They were afraid of getting
kicked out of the meeting place. When push came
to shove they cared more for human approval than
for God's glory.

Matthew 10:32-33 Good News Translation
32 "Those who declare publicly that they belong
to me, I will do the same for them before my

Father in heaven. 33 But those who reject me publicly, I will reject before my Father in heaven. The people who are brought back in this resurrection have turned their backs on God and Jesus. It is not for those who backslide and repent later. These are the ones who choose sin wilfully, following in the example of Satan. All will have to give an account for themselves and be judged. Having been resurrected as mortal beings when thrown into the lake of fire they will be destroyed and die.

Revelation 20:11-15 King James Version
11 And I saw a great white throne, and him that sat on it, from whose face the earth and the heaven fled away; and there was found no place for them.
12 And I saw the dead, small and great, stand before God; and the books were opened: and another book was opened, which is the book of life: and the dead were judged out of those things which were written in the books, according to their works.
13 And the sea gave up the dead which were in it; and death and hell delivered up the dead which

were in them: and they were judged every man according to their works.

14 And death and hell were cast into the lake of fire. This is the second death.

15 And whosoever was not found written in the book of life was cast into the lake of fire.

They may know Jesus and be fully expecting to enter into God's Kingdom only to find they have been rejected.

Matthew 7:21-23 Easy-to-Read Version

21 "Not everyone who calls me Lord will enter God's Kingdom. The only people who will enter are those who do what my Father in heaven wants. 22 On that last Day many will call me Lord. They will say, 'Lord, Lord, by the power of your name we spoke for God. And by your name we forced out demons and did many miracles.' 23 Then I will tell those people clearly, 'Get away from me, you people who do wrong. I never knew you.'

Matthew 13:24-30 Living Bible

24 Here is another illustration Jesus used: "The Kingdom of Heaven is like a farmer sowing good

seed in his field; 25 but one night as he slept, his enemy came and sowed thistles among the wheat. 26 When the crop began to grow, the thistles grew too.

27 "The farmer's men came and told him, 'Sir, the field where you planted that choice seed is full of thistles!'

28 "'An enemy has done it,' he exclaimed.

"'Shall we pull out the thistles?' they asked.

29 "'No,' he replied. 'You'll hurt the wheat if you do. 30 Let both grow together until the harvest, and I will tell the reapers to sort out the thistles and burn them, and put the wheat in the barn.'"

When people accept the salvation brought by Jesus and become Christians they are responsible for their own actions. God expects them to grow in the fruit of the Spirit, becoming the best they can, growing as fruitful as possible. The investment or down payment of the Holy Spirit that God gives us needs to grow so that when Jesus returns there will be an increase.

Matthew 25:14-30 English Standard Version
14 "For it will be like a man going on a journey,

who called his servants and entrusted to them his property. 15 To one he gave five talents, to another two, to another one, to each according to his ability. Then he went away. 16 He who had received the five talents went at once and traded with them, and he made five talents more. 17 So also he who had the two talents made two talents more. 18 But he who had received the one talent went and dug in the ground and hid his master's money. 19 Now after a long time the master of those servants came and settled accounts with them. 20 And he who had received the five talents came forward, bringing five talents more, saying, 'Master, you delivered to me five talents; here I have made five talents more.' 21 His master said to him, 'Well done, good and faithful servant. You have been faithful over a little; I will set you over much. Enter into the joy of your master.' 22 And he also who had the two talents came forward, saying, 'Master, you delivered to me two talents; here I have made two talents more.' 23 His master said to him, 'Well done, good and faithful servant. You have been faithful over a little; I will set you over much. Enter into the joy of your master.' 24 He also who had received the one talent came forward, saying, 'Master, I knew you to be a hard man, reaping where you did not sow, and gathering where you scattered no seed, 25 so I was afraid, and I went and hid your talent in the ground. Here you have what is yours.' 26 But his master answered him, 'You wicked and slothful servant! You knew that I reap where I have not sown and gather where I scattered no seed? 27 Then you ought to have invested my money with the bankers, and at my coming I should have received what was my own with interest. 28 So take the talent from him and give it to him who has the ten talents. 29 For to everyone who has will more be given, and he will have an abundance. But from the one who has not, even what he has will be taken away. 30 And cast the worthless servant into the outer darkness. In that place there will be weeping and gnashing of teeth.'

How we are rewarded will play out differently for each person, it will depend on where and how you follow the Spirits lead. The example of all of those who went before us is there for our encouragement. It's not for someone else to tell you how to follow, they may give advice, but it's up to each and every Christian to finish the race on the track set before them. God has set us on a path that will lead us to him. He desires us to become active participants in the Kingdom with him and will give us the strength to get there. All we have to do is have the will and courage to follow.

Hebrews 12:1-3 Good News Translation
1 As for us, we have this large crowd of witnesses around us. So then, let us rid ourselves of everything that gets in the way, and of the sin which holds on to us so tightly, and let us run with determination the race that lies before us. 2 Let us keep our eyes fixed on Jesus, on whom our faith depends from beginning to end. He did not give up because of the cross! On the contrary, because of the joy that was waiting for him, he thought nothing of the disgrace of dying on the cross, and he is now seated at the right side of God's throne. 3 Think of what he went through; how he put up with so much hatred from sinners! So do not let yourselves become discouraged and give up.

The punishment for those not found in the book of life is being thrown into the lake of fire. This is the second death from which there is no resurrection. They will be dead for the rest of eternity, their punishment will be eternal. Having had their opportunity to choose and follow Jesus they either rejected it, or quit before the end. They will reap the rewards of their choices and their choices will be respected for the rest of time.

Malachi 4:1-3 Easy-to-Read Version
1 "That time of judgment is coming. It will be like a hot furnace. All the proud people will be punished. All the evil people will burn like straw. At that time they will be like a bush burning in the fire, and there will not be a branch or root left." This is what the Lord All-Powerful said. 2 "But, for my followers, goodness will shine on you like the rising sun. And it will bring healing power like the sun's rays. You will be free and happy, like calves freed from their stalls. 3 Then you will walk on the evil people—they will be like ashes under your feet. I will make this happen at the time of judgment." This is what the Lord All-Powerful said.

2 Thessalonians 1:8-9 Good News Translation
8 with a flaming fire, to punish those who reject
God and who do not obey the Good News about
our Lord Jesus. 9 They will suffer the punishment
of eternal destruction, separated from the presence
of the Lord and from his glorious might,

Being mortal man they can only live in a physical
world. If their physical surroundings don't support
life then they will die. A spiritual life is only
possible through the power of God's Holy Spirit.
Having made the choice to reject, or spurn God's
free gift of spiritual life, and have real life to the
full, no further redemption for them is possible.

Genesis 6:3 Good News Translation
3 Then the Lord said, "I will not allow people to
live forever; they are mortal. From now on they
will live no longer than 120 years."

John 3:16 King James Version
16 For God so loved the world, that he gave his
only begotten Son, that whosoever believeth in
him should not perish, but have everlasting life.

Hebrews 6:4-8 The Message

4-8 Once people have seen the light, gotten a taste of heaven and been part of the work of the Holy Spirit, once they've personally experienced the sheer goodness of God's Word and the powers breaking in on us—if then they turn their backs on it, washing their hands of the whole thing, well, they can't start over as if nothing happened. That's impossible. Why, they've re-crucified Jesus! They've repudiated him in public! Parched ground that soaks up the rain and then produces an abundance of carrots and corn for its gardener gets God's "Well done!" But if it produces weeds and thistles, it's more likely to get cussed out. Fields like that are burned, not harvested.

Lastly death and hell are cast into the lake of fire. They are the final enemies to be conquered. Now all who ever lived will have had their chance to either accept or reject God and the deliverance brought to them through Jesus. All people will be given one opportunity to follow Jesus, some if they are called by God have that chance in this life. The others who are not called for whatever reason will get their chance through one of the resurrections.

Finally after all adversaries are gone, after all who are left have said yes, we want to live with God in his loving ways, God will bring his Kingdom to us and we will live with him forever as his children.

Revelation 21:1-7 King James Version
1 And I saw a new heaven and a new earth: for the first heaven and the first earth were passed away; and there was no more sea.
2 And I John saw the holy city, new Jerusalem, coming down from God out of heaven, prepared as a bride adorned for her husband.
3 And I heard a great voice out of heaven saying, Behold, the tabernacle of God is with men, and he will dwell with them, and they shall be his people, and God himself shall be with them, and be their God.
4 And God shall wipe away all tears from their eyes; and there shall be no more death, neither sorrow, nor crying, neither shall there be any more pain: for the former things are passed away.

5 And he that sat upon the throne said, Behold, I make all things new. And he said unto me, Write: for these words are true and faithful.

6 And he said unto me, It is done. I am Alpha and Omega, the beginning and the end. I will give unto him that is athirst of the fountain of the water of life freely.

7 He that overcometh shall inherit all things; and I will be his God, and he shall be my son.

John gives us a glimpse of what our heavenly home will look like.

Revelation 21:9-27 The Message

9-12 One of the Seven Angels who had carried the bowls filled with the seven final disasters spoke to me: "Come here. I'll show you the Bride, the Wife of the Lamb." He took me away in the Spirit to an enormous, high mountain and showed me Holy Jerusalem descending out of Heaven from God, resplendent in the bright glory of God.

12-14 The City shimmered like a precious gem, light-filled, pulsing light. She had a wall majestic and high with twelve gates. At each gate stood an Angel, and on the gates were inscribed the names of the Twelve Tribes of the sons of Israel: three gates on the east, three gates on the north, three gates on the south, three gates on the west. The wall was set on twelve foundations, the names of the Twelve Apostles of the Lamb inscribed on them.

15-21 The Angel speaking with me had a gold measuring stick to measure the City, its gates, and its wall. The City was laid out in a perfect square. He measured the City with the measuring stick: twelve thousand stadia, its length, width, and height all equal. Using the standard measure, the Angel measured the thickness of its wall: 144 cubits. The wall was jasper, the color of Glory, and the City was pure gold, translucent as glass. The foundations of the City walls were garnished with every precious gem imaginable: the first foundation jasper, the second sapphire, the third agate, the fourth emerald, the fifth onyx, the sixth carnelian, the seventh chrysolite, the eighth beryl, the ninth topaz, the tenth chrysoprase, the eleventh jacinth, the twelfth amethyst. The twelve gates were twelve pearls, each gate a single pearl.

21-27 The main street of the City was pure gold, translucent as glass. But there was no sign of a Temple, for the Lord God—the Sovereign-

Strong—and the Lamb are the Temple. The City doesn't need sun or moon for light. God's Glory is its light, the Lamb its lamp! The nations will walk in its light and earth's kings bring in their splendor. Its gates will never be shut by day, and there won't be any night. They'll bring the glory and honor of the nations into the City. Nothing dirty or defiled will get into the City, and no one who defiles or deceives. Only those whose names are written in the Lamb's Book of Life will get in.

What our new bodies will be like is yet unknown to us. We can only speculate. From our vantage point on this side of glory, it is hard to make out the shape of our spirit life to come.

1Corinthians 13:12 New International Version
12 For now we see only a reflection as in a mirror; then we shall see face to face. Now I know in part; then I shall know fully, even as I am fully known.

1 Corinthians 15:49 Living Bible
49 Just as each of us now has a body like Adam's, so we shall someday have a body like Christ's.

Even though we don't know all the details of God's plan, he has given us enough information to give us hope and let us dream of what splendours await us. Staying focused on who we are in the family of God and the vital roles we have in the Kingdom is crucial if we are to run our race well. Having a quest and a purpose for our lives larger than anything this world can offer gives us joy and contentment. There is a sure outcome waiting for those who reject the things of the world. Our prize is not an earthly one that will fade with time but rather it is one that will last forever.

1Corinthians 9:24-27 The Voice
24 We all know that when there's a race, all the runners bolt for the finish line, but only one will take the prize. When you run, run for the prize! 25 Athletes in training are very strict with themselves, exercising self-control over desires, and for what? For a wreath that soon withers or is crushed or simply forgotten. That is not our race. We run for the crown that we will wear for eternity. 26 So I don't run aimlessly. I don't let my eyes drift off the finish line. When I box, I don't throw punches in the air. 27 I discipline my

body and make it my slave so that after all this, after I have brought the gospel to others, I will still be qualified to win the prize.

The Kingdom of God will finally be here in its fullness. I think that Handles Messiah will be the theme song for the whole world as the new Jerusalem is ushered in and we see our new home. God has an incredible future in store for his children. Hallelujah!

2 Corinthians 4:17 New Life Version
17 The little troubles we suffer now for a short time are making us ready for the great things God is going to give us forever.

1 Corinthians 2:9 New King James Version
9 But as it is written: "Eye has not seen, nor ear heard, Nor have entered into the heart of man The things which God has prepared for those who love Him."

Armed with the fruit of the Holy Spirit we will live the full and abundant life that God has been waiting to spend with us. Out of all the fruit we can produce, we should be sure to have love as our best, for it is love that will last the longest.

1 Corinthians 13:7-13 J.B. Phillips New Testament

7-8a Love knows no limit to its endurance, no end to its trust, no fading of its hope; it can outlast anything. It is, in fact, the one thing that still stands when all else has fallen.

8b-10 For if there are prophecies they will be fulfilled and done with, if there are "tongues" the need for them will disappear, if there is knowledge it will be swallowed up in truth. For our knowledge is always incomplete and our prophecy is always incomplete, and when the complete comes, that is the end of the incomplete.

11 When I was a little child I talked and felt and thought like a little child. Now that I am a man my childish speech and feeling and thought have no further significance for me.

12 At present we are men looking at puzzling reflections in a mirror. The time will come when we shall see reality whole and face to face! At present all I know is a little fraction of the truth, but the time will come when I shall know it as

fully as God now knows me!

13 In this life we have three great lasting qualities—faith, hope and love. But the greatest of them is love.

Growing fruit of the Spirit is not always an easy process. It can be painful and will go against our human nature.

1Peter 2:20 King James Version

20 For what glory is it, if, when ye be buffeted for your faults, ye shall take it patiently? but if, when ye do well, and suffer for it, ye take it patiently, this is acceptable with God.

Having faith in God and understanding the plan of salvation he is bringing to the world aids us in not only making disciples but in proclaiming the Kingdom to a weary world. Knowing how and when all of humanity will have an opportunity to come to Jesus and then the father, makes the message of Christianity hopeful and inclusive. Telling people they can only get to God through Jesus, which is true, but not telling them that they must be called by God to get to Jesus is, in my opinion, misleading and exclusive.

John 14:6 New Life Version
6 Jesus said, "I am the Way and the Truth and the Life. No one can go to the Father except by Me.

John 6:44 New International Version
44 "No one can come to me unless the Father who sent me draws them, and I will raise them up at the last day.

Knowing the plan for mankind's salvation is essential if we are to offer God's hope to those who are grieving the loss of a loved one that did not know Jesus. Whether it was a child's untimely death or an adult's, knowing that God has a plan where all will have an opportunity to freely accept the sacrifice of Jesus can be the difference between despair and hopefulness.

Isaiah 26:19 Good News Translation
19 Those of our people who have died will live again! Their bodies will come back to life. All those sleeping in their graves will wake up and sing for joy. As the sparkling dew refreshes the earth, so the Lord will revive those who have long

been dead.

Hebrews 8:11 Jubilee Bible 2000
11 and no one shall teach his neighbour nor
anyone his brother, saying, Know the Lord, for all
shall know me, from the least to the greatest.

God desires people who want to be with him, not
people looking to escape the punishment of hell.
Choosing God only as the better of two options
would leave some that chose God not fully
committed to him. They would choose him, not
out of love, but out of fear.

John 14:21 Living Bible
21 The one who obeys me is the one who loves
me; and because he loves me, my Father will love
him; and I will too, and I will reveal myself to
him."

The resurrections bring hope to humanity, not so
that they will get another chance at living a Godly
life. The hope of the resurrections is that all
people will receive one chance to choose Jesus.
All of those who never received the call of God,

those who were blinded so they could not see, had their ears plugged so they could not hear and had their hearts hardened so they would not accept the love of God. They will have their opportunity to freely come to the God who loves them. That opportunity will occur through the resurrections.

Some Christians may ask, "why should I suffer now if I could have it easier later"? They forget that the blessings of being called by God now outweigh the troubles. I ask them, "did you follow Jesus because you wanted to escape hell, were you looking for an easy life with riches or did you follow Jesus, as the apostles did, because you couldn't live without him"?

John 6:68-69 J.B. Phillips New Testament
68-69 "Lord," answered Simon Peter, "who else should we go to? Your words have the ring of eternal life! And we believe and are convinced that you are the holy one of God."
We all should follow Jesus not for the rewards in this life, but for our future rewards of an eternal life of love. We will all receive the same payment for our labour. God will reward each Christian as

he sees fit. Our lives are not ours for we sold ourselves to Jesus and we were bought for a price. Each must follow where his master leads them in their own race.

John 21:22 Easy-to-Read Version
22 Jesus answered, "Maybe I want him to live until I come. That should not matter to you. You follow me!"

Romans 6:16-18 New Living Translation
16 Don't you realize that you become the slave of whatever you choose to obey? You can be a slave to sin, which leads to death, or you can choose to obey God, which leads to righteous living. 17 Thank God! Once you were slaves of sin, but now you wholeheartedly obey this teaching we have given you. 18 Now you are free from your slavery to sin, and you have become slaves to righteous living.

We who are called now in this present life are called by God to fulfil his will. Christians need to follow the Holy Spirit where it leads them, growing the best crop of spiritual fruit they can.

Now is our day of salvation, we have to make our election sure. If we fail we will lose out on the blessings God has in store for us and be burned in the lake of fire. Our chance for salvation is now. Our time to grow in love that will last for eternity are in the struggles of this life.

The Kingdom of God is coming to us in God's good time. We need only to proclaim it to the world by our words and deeds. God will call those who he wants to Jesus. We are to help make them his disciples through instruction and example, lovingly teaching them all that Jesus has instructed us. These instructions are contained in the word of god, the bible. Growing the fruit of the spirit now is vital for our lives to come in the Kingdom. Like Jesus was, we need to be about our fathers business during this life, making ours an election sure.

Luke 12:36-40 New International Version
36 like servants waiting for their master to return from a wedding banquet, so that when he comes and knocks they can immediately open the door for him. 37 It will be good for those servants

whose master finds them watching when he comes. Truly I tell you, he will dress himself to serve, will have them recline at the table and will come and wait on them. 38 It will be good for those servants whose master finds them ready, even if he comes in the middle of the night or toward daybreak. 39 But understand this: If the owner of the house had known at what hour the thief was coming, he would not have let his house be broken into. 40 You also must be ready, because the Son of Man will come at an hour when you do not expect him.

CONNECT WITH CLAYTON CARLSON

I really appreciate you reading my book!

Friend me on Facebook:
https://www.facebook.com/biblists
Visit my website: http://www.biblists.com/

Other books by Clayton B Carlson

Biblist Apologetics
My Baby Died. Where is My Baby?
Searching For Immortality
The Eden Conspiracy
Thy Kingdom Come, The Next Big Thing.

ABOUT THE AUTHOR

Clayton and his wife live in the Okanagan Valley of southern British Colombia, Canada. They have two adult children and enjoy getting out to explore the outdoors, camping and quading. Clayton started his working career as an owner-operator in the trucking industry. After an industrial accident he retrained as a heavy duty mechanic and driving instructor. He enjoys working with his hands. Being a tradesman provides a good living for his family, but his passion is to study the Bible as the Bereans did, proving what is true from the scriptures.

Clayton is a published freelance author within the Christian genre. He writes articles and bible studies for the www.Biblists.com web site, and has audio books and articles appearing on various podcast websites.

Join Clayton and team in the Berean tradition, as they find biblical truth. Understanding scripture by reviewing original texts of ancient believers, scrutinizing modern theology.

www.ingramcontent.com/pod-product-compliance
Lightning Source LLC
Chambersburg PA
CBHW060038040426
42331CB00032B/1057